VOLUME THREE

The Rite of Penance: Commentaries

Background and Directions

Nathan Mitchell, OSB, editor

Godfrey Diekmann, OSB
Cora Marie Dubitsky
Colman Grabert, OSB
Raymond Studzinski, OSB

1978 THE LITURGICAL CONFERENCE
WASHINGTON, D.C.

THE LITURGICAL CONFERENCE
1221 Massachusetts Avenue, N.W.
Washington, D.C. 20005

THE RITE OF PENANCE: COMMENTARIES is a series that includes, in addition to this volume, *Volume I: Understanding the Document,* by Ralph Keifer and Frederick R. McManus, and *Volume II: Implementing the Rite,* edited by Elizabeth McMahon Jeep.

Library of Congress Catalog Card No. 75-42590
ISBN 0-918208-09-2
First Printing, June 1978

Contents

Introduction

Nearly five years have elapsed since the Congregation for Divine Worship published the *Rite of Penance,* reformed by mandate of the Second Vatican Council. During these years pastors and theologians, liturgists and religious educators have been challenged to re-evaluate the Christian ministry of reconciliation. Quite clearly that ministry is not limited to the forum of sacramental penance, for reconciliation lies at the very heart of the New Testament's many-faceted message about the peace bestowed on humanity through the blood of Jesus' cross. The essays collected in this volume explore the theme of reconciliation not only as it appears in the new rites of penance but also as it emerges in other contexts, e.g., in the celebration of the eucharist and in the community's life of intercession and prayer.

Common to all these essays is the conviction that reconciliation can be sought and discovered in a *variety* of ways. For centuries the Catholic tradition has esteemed sacramental penance in the form of "private confession." While this individual form of celebration continues to offer Christians valuable opportunities for growth in faith, it has never been the *exclusive* avenue to reconciliation. History reveals that the discipline and pastoral practice of penance have been shaped by the changing circumstances of Christian life in the world. In every age Christians have acknowledged that their community is simultaneously holy and sinful— and this acknowledgement has led to a search for new ways to proclaim God's word of forgiveness, a word ever new and ever renewed.

The essays offered here are evidence of the church's continuing quest for repentance and conversion. The contributors have approached the task of evaluating the new rites of penance from several different perspectives: biblical studies, the history of Christian worship, sacramental theology, religious education and systematic theology. It has been their intention not merely to comment on the rites but to raise questions and identify issues that need discussion as Christians continue the ministry of reconciliation.

Special thanks are due to Robert W. Hovda, Melissa Kay and Mary C. Maher of The Liturgical Conference for generous assistance in the preparation of this volume. Their vigorous dedication to the quality of Christian prayer and worship has made the task of editing these essays a rare pleasure.

Nathan Mitchell, O.S.B.
St. Meinrad Archabbey
St. Meinrad, Indiana

Eastertide, 1978

CHAPTER ONE

Conversion and Reconciliation in the New Testament: The Parable of the Cross

Nathan Mitchell, OSB

"A quilt is something human." That's what Brooks Eliot Wigginton tells us in *The Foxfire Book* (Wigginton, 1972, 142). In the Appalachian region of America, quilt making, quilting bees and quilting parties are significant social occasions, bright times that bring people together. As Wigginton remarks: "The simple fact is that quilts were handmade by people for people. Every phase of their production was permeated by giving and sharing. From the trading of scraps and patterns and the actual production in 'bees' to the giving away of the final finished work, quilting was an essentially human activity. There is something about a quilt that says people, friendship, community, family, home, and love" (Wigginton 1972, 144). A quilt is something human. It's an intriguing answer to an ancient question posed time and again by thinkers: what makes people human? What makes people distinctive, different from the myriad other forms of life which swarm over the planet?

Every age has a new answer to this perpetually vexing question. The answers are never very satisfying, but that is unimportant. What *is* important is the effort to keep struggling with the question. Thus, some anthropologists today would argue that what makes people human is the ability to make and keep tools—tools which stretch and extend the human senses and permit us to develop technologies. The camera, for example, stretches the human eye, allows it to intrude on privacies that would otherwise remain unobserved and unknown. The stethoscope stretches the human ear, lets us hear how the heart and lungs are behaving. The smoke detector in a large office building stretches the human nose, helps it discover hazardous fumes that can cause illness and death. All these technological extensions of the human sensory apparatus contribute to the creation of a specifically *human* environment, one in which human life can be sustained, developed and, presumably, improved.

The anthropologists are probably right. Tools made and kept, tested and improved upon, do contribute to the world we identify as distinctively human. But there is another answer, a humbler one, to the ques-

1

tion "what makes people people?" It is an answer almost as old as humanity itself: the power of language—the power to *tell stories*. The human world is, as Professor Brian Wicker has observed, a "story-shaped world" (Wicker, 1975). People do not simply tell stories, they *live* in the stories they tell. A story is more than a "good yarn," an intriguing tale brilliantly told; it is a good place to live, a necessary human environment. Story is, in fact, the biography of the race. We live in layers of story spun through centuries by poets, known and unknown, by witty court jesters, by nameless hunters who sat by night fires telling tales of animals hunted and snared. These stories *are* our world. They tell us, as Franz Kafka once suggested, that the difference between being *dreamed* and being *real* is very slight.

Stories, then, are something human. We live in the thick of them, we repeat and alter them, develop new ones and remember old ones. But if human persons have the power to tell stories, stories also have the power to *tell us*. We are shaped, changed, transformed and sometimes victimized by stories. The story of humanity as tool-making and tool-keeping is a good illustration of this point. The telling of this story has produced men and women who are technocrats, creatures who derive voluptuous power from the tools they produce and hoard. This is a story of human intelligence and daring, but it is also a story of economic arrogance and wanton wastefulness. So great is the power of the story, however, that in the face of it human beings can become infinitely gullible. For example, the story of unalterable human progress—every day in every way things are getting better and better—still captivates most of us from time to time, even as we read terrifying stories about neutron bombs and paralyzing gases for use in modern warfare.

Jesus as a Storyteller

If storytelling is a distinctively human activity, it should not surprise us to find that Jesus is portrayed in the New Testament as a master of the story. Jesus not only told stories in his own ministry of preaching the kingdom, but he himself became the central tale of Christian faith: the storyteller became the story! Indeed, writers like the late J.R.R. Tolkien, whose *Lord of the Rings* has become a modern classic, have regarded the gospels as story in its highest form. The gospels, Tolkien once remarked, are the supreme example of the "eucatastrophe"—the story with a sudden joyous turn, the tale that begins and ends in happiness (Tolkien 1966, 71-72). For the gospel-story has redeemed the human imagination once and for all. As Tolkien put it: " . . . in God's kingdom the presence of the greatest does not depress the small. Redeemed Man is still man. Story, fantasy, still go on, and should go on. The gospel has not abrogated legends; it has hallowed them, especially the 'happy ending.' The Christian has still to work, with mind as well as body, to suffer, hope, and die; but he may now perceive that all his bents and faculties have a purpose, which can be redeemed . . . All tales may come true" (Tolkien 1966, 72-73).

If Jesus was a storyteller—and if he has become the supreme story of Christian believers—then it is important for us to know what kind of stories he told. The ancient world, after all, swarmed with men and women who spun tales of time and eternity. Epic poets like Homer and Vergil told panoramic stories about the origin and history of heroes. Anonymous balladeers sang mysterious songs about how the earth and humanity came to be: "At the time when Yahweh God made earth and heaven, there was as yet no wild bush on the earth nor had any wild plant yet sprung up, for Yahweh God had not sent rain on the earth, nor was there any man to till the soil. However, a flood was rising from the earth and watering all the surface of the soil. Yahweh God fashioned man of dust from the soil. Then he breathed into his nostrils a breath of life, and thus man became a living being" (Genesis 2:5-7). Stories and songs like these have continued to be repeated through the centuries; we live in them, stretch and walk about in their thick crusted layers. Jesus, however, was not a man who was content simply to repeat the traditional wisdom and folklore of his people. His stories were "different"—and it is the difference that concerns us here.

New Testament scholars have repeatedly reminded us during the past several years that Jesus often used a form of story called "parable." Of itself this is no great surprise. Prominent rabbis liked to illustrate their teaching with stories which drew on familiar human experiences of nature (seeds and sowers; animals and agriculture) and personality (marriage and children; crooks and charlatans; kings and subjects). Jesus did not invent parables; they were known and used by wise men before him. But as Jesus used them, the parables were transformed. A new twist was added to the story—one that was often unexpected, shocking and even subversive. Instead of being colorful illustrations cleverly used to emphasize a point of teaching, Jesus' parables caught his hearers off guard, left them "hanging." Anyone who has ever seen an Alfred Hitchcock film or television series will know the feeling. Beneath its superficial horror, for example, Hitchcock's film, *The Birds,* leaves one with the unsettling question: what if that were true? What if all those friendly flocks of wrens and robins were secretly hatching a plot to attack people? Hitchcock's films don't provide answers; they raise frustrating questions, they confront us with uncomfortable possibilities and doubts. Leaving the theatre after such a film, we have the disquieting sense that the story "didn't turn out right," that it left something unsaid or what is said is something we did not want nor expect to hear.

In this sense, the parables, as Jesus used them, resemble a Hitchcock film. They are short on answers and long on strange twists which subvert our expectations. The parable of the Good Samaritan is a well-known example. As this story stands in the New Testament (Luke 10: 25-37), it has been transformed into a tale about good moral example. A Jewish man has been criminally abused, injured and left for dead. After a priest and a Levite pass by without helping him, a Samaritan comes to his rescue. The implication? We should follow that Samaritan's example: "Jesus said, 'Go, and do the same yourselves'" (Luke 10:37). The evangelist Luke has edited the parable, changing it into a story of exemplary moral conduct; it has become a lesson in how Christian disciples ought to behave when they meet misery and misfortune—even in their enemies.

Scholars have shown, however, that the original form of the Good Samaritan parable was far more disquieting. It must be remembered that in Jesus' day Jews and Samaritans did not get along well; each regarded the other as despicable. The strange twist in the story as Jesus told it was not that one man helped another who was in trouble, but that a *Samaritan* generously came to the aid of a *Jew.* To the people of Jesus' time this would have been shocking, unthinkable, scandalous. Perhaps we could get a sense of the parable's unexpected shock if we substituted different names for Jew and Samaritan. How would the story sound, for example, if the injured party were Anita Bryant and the generous helper were a man just returning from the neighborhood gay bar? The point of the parable is precisely that it subverts our ordinary expectations and forces us to rethink our common assumptions about good and bad people, morality and immorality, virtue and sin. As Jesus told the original parable his hearers were caught off guard. Before they knew what was happening, they found themselves challenged by an unexpected possibility: a repulsive Samaritan could be a good and generous man.

In the ministry of Jesus, moreover, the parables sometimes took the form of *deeds,* provocative and unexpected actions. Jesus' association with the group known as "tax-collectors" provides a good example here. As John Dominic Crossan has noted, the "tax-collectors" spoken of in the literature of the New Testament were actually "*toll*-collectors," men who collected the indirect taxes or tolls from citizens (Crossan 1975, 90-91). The system of tolls easily bred greed and dishonesty; it was tempting to fleece the public by padding the tolls and pocketing the surcharge. The injustice of this system is obvious; it amounted to theft, and the people were often helpless to resist the toll-collector's power. Jesus, the gospels tell us, shamelessly shared table fellowship with these notoriously fraudulent folks (see Luke 5:29-32). In the eyes of many of his contemporaries, Jesus' behavior was scandalously unacceptable. A true prophet of God would not sit at table with men who lied, cheated and stole from the poor. For to break bread with another is to share the staff of life, to enter into a relationship of communion with him. What did Jesus' action mean? Was he winking at injustice, cooperating with fraud and deception? If Jesus were a holy man approved by God would he hobnob with these corrupt crooks? Once again, we might substitute contemporary figures for the toll-collectors. What if Jesus frequented elegant restaurants like the *Sans Souci* in the company of Tongsun Park? Behavior of this sort would not only raise eyebrows, it would arouse justifiable anger and dismay. Jesus' parabolic deed of eating with toll-collectors (equals "sinners") deliberately provoked the most disconcerting questions. What is this man up to? How can he justify going out on the town with cheap criminals and detestable gangsters?

Sometimes, too, Jesus' parable-stories poked fun at sacred institutions and holy customs. It is unfortunate that we have lost contact with the satirical humor of Jesus' teaching. We think of him as the most serious of men, soberly stalking around Palestine with pursed lips, a rock-like chin and a hard glint in his eye. The parables, however, reveal Jesus' considerable talent as a satirist. His ironic sense of humor was not unlike that of Gary Trudeau, whose "Doonesbury" cartoons lampoon all sorts of sacred cows. Take the parable of the mustard seed as an example. John Dominic Crossan has shown that Jesus' description of the kingdom of heaven as a mustard seed (Luke 13:18-19) is a humorous satire on traditional biblical images (Crossan 1975, 93-96). The mustard plant is, after all, a rather miserable little bush. Even today, farmers find it a nuisance because it grows wild and rapidly, thus choking off the life of other crops. And, in any case, the mustard plant is a runt when compared to something as grand as a towering "cedar of Lebanon," the image used by Ezekiel, for example, to describe the mighty people of the messianic kingdom (Ezekiel 17:22-23; see Crossan 1975, 94-95). Once more the parable is provocative; it subverts our expectations. What are we to think? Is the *kingdom*—God's ultimate act of blessing for humanity—nothing more than a puny nuisance like the mustard plant? Is God that helpless and ineffective? Is the kingdom no more impressive than Charlie Brown's Christmas tree—a scrawny branch with two pieces of tinsel and a shattered glass ornament? If that's all the kingdom is, then why wait or hope or pray for it?

Like Hitchcock's films, Jesus' parables seem to be stories that "turn out wrong," stories with strange ironic twists which take us to places we don't want to go. Ultimately, of course, Jesus himself became the most puzzling parable of all. The cross is the final satire on human expectations. It subverts the last shred of common sense assumptions about how God works in the world. In the cross much of the messianic project collapses in twisted failure and death. The disappointment is brutal and complete. The storyteller dies with words of incomprehension and shrieking despair on his lips. We are left holding the bag, caught off guard. The carefully constructed world of our stories, the world in which God blesses good men and vindicates prophets, buckles and begins to crumble. The cross calls all our stories into question, makes us wonder if any of them are true. In the face of death's finality, all our defensive stories about God's "will" and "plan" become nonsensical. How can the God of the living "will" the death of people who served him faithfully? What if the world really is senseless and absurd? What if our self-assured stories about the meaning of life are ridiculous deceptions or illusions we create in order to stave off the terror of emptiness and futility? In the cross all these questions come howling into our consciousness, demanding answers where there are no answers.

The Parable of the Cross and the Challenge of Conversion

The subversive parable of the cross makes one thing clear: Jesus cannot be understood as simply a Palestinian Aristotle, a peripetetic teacher of ethics who encouraged people to seek good and avoid evil. Jesus offers no definitions of ethical goodness; if anything, his parables challenge common human expectations about good and bad behavior. This is a point that is difficult for most of us to understand. We are so accustomed to badmouthing the Pharisees that when Jesus says that "prostitutes and sinners are closer to the kingdom than they," we nod our heads approvingly and assume we know exactly what is meant. We forget that in Jesus' day the Pharisees were not the frenzied band of bigots later Christian history has made them out to be. One of several religious and political parties in Palestine during Jesus' lifetime, the Pharisees represented some of the finest Jewish traditions of scholarship, devotion to God's Word, and moral wisdom. Nor were the Pharisees narrow-minded ogres who claimed an absolute monopoly on religious truth. As Paul Winter has written: "It is wrong to think that the Pharisees as a body promised a share in the blessedness of the next world only to Israelites. 'The rightteous of all peoples share in the world to come' runs a frequently quoted saying of the rabbis. The Pharisees preached penitence and repentance of sin as the way of bringing in the kingdom of God. . . . This conviction explains why the Pharisees made such efforts to obey God completely. Fulfilling the law was never for them a matter of external observance only" (Winter 1971, 53). Indeed, of all the sectarian groups represented in Palestine during Jesus' time, the Pharisees were probably closest to him in religious outlook (see Winter 1971, 51-52).

Too often Christians attempt to interpret the gospel message of conversion and kingdom by opposing it to "Pharisaic legalism." It is assumed that Jesus preached a kingdom accessible through *interior* conversion of heart, while the Pharisees announced the coming of God's reign exclusively for those devoted to *external works* of the Law. This contrast is erroneous and drastically misleading. Like most sensitive religious thinkers, the great Pharisaic rabbis were keenly aware of the tragedy of humankind's relationship to God. They knew how vulnerable the human spirit can be, how fickle and devious the heart can become. They also knew that human beings have to *act* and to *do penance* if they are to come to grips with the challenge of fidelity to the God of the covenant and his promises. That is why the rabbinic teachers in the tradition of Pharisaism used to say things like "When the Israelites do penance they are redeemed," and "It is not discussion that is important but action" (Winter 1971, 53, 56).

It would be a mistake, therefore, to underestimate the radical challenge of conversion already present in the Pharisaic tradition at the time of Jesus. The idea that nobody ever thought about conversion of heart until John the Baptist, Jesus and Paul appeared on the scene is utterly absurd. Conversion of heart is, after all, one of the central themes of prophetic literature in the Hebrew Bible. Consider, for example, this text from the prophet Jeremiah: "Deep within them I will plant my Law, writing it on their hearts. Then I will be their God and they will be my people. There will be no further need for neighbour to try to teach neighbour, or brother to say to brother, 'Learn to know Yahweh!' No, they will all know me, the least no less than the greatest—it is Yahweh who speaks—since I will forgive their iniquity and never call their sin to mind" (Jeremiah 31:33-34).

Jesus' teaching about conversion and kingdom cannot, then, be understood as a "call to interiorization" in a religious world which thought only in terms of legal prescriptions, cultic regulations and external observances. Nor can we think of Jesus' message as an "ethics of the heart," as opposed to a presumed Pharisaic "ethics of Law."

7

What, then, is the sense of conversion found in the message of the New Testament? *Metanoia,* the Greek term usually translated by the English words "repentance" or "conversion," occurs frequently in the Synoptic gospels, often in the imperative verb form (*metanoeite*: "Repent!"). Literally, *metanoia* means "to change one's mind." But there is danger that for modern readers "changing one's mind" may be taken to mean a weak, almost capricious change of "attitude." For us, the expression "I've changed my mind" may refer to a spur-of-the-moment decision, a sudden whim. In the New Testament, however, the language of conversion has nothing to do with the whimsical change of a person's emotional climate. The language of conversion is part of a larger language: Jesus' proclamation of the *kingdom* that is both "at hand" and "yet to come." As strange as it may sound, the New Testament language of *metanoia* has little to do with the doctrines of ethics or moral theology. Repentance and conversion are far more radical than discussions about birth-control or masturbation. The challenge of conversion is not the challenge of accepting Jesus ethical teaching, but the more basic challenge of *recognizing God at work in the world,* establishing a kingdom (or "reign") which is surprising, unexpected and even scandalous. The crisis provoked by Jesus through his teaching and ministry was not the crisis of a new ethical system but a crisis of *recognition.* By means of parabolic deeds and stories, Jesus challenged his hearers to *recognize* the reign of God that was breaking into the world in his own person—in the person of a carpenter's son, a man who loved prostitutes and sat at table with toll-collectors, a man who used gentle irony to puncture the arrogance of sacred customs and holy traditions. "Repent!" means to *recognize* in Jesus of Nazareth the ultimate manifestation of God's sovereign action in the world.

According to the late biblical scholar Norman Perrin, the challenge of conversion in the New Testament can be summarized in the words "recognition and response" (Perrin 1967, 109-153). If we are looking for blazing new ethical insights from the gospels, Perrin suggests, we will be disappointed: " . . . 'ethics' is a misleading word, because it carries with it the assumption that there is a Christian ethic as there is a Socratic or humanistic ethic. So far as the teaching of Jesus is concerned, this latter is simply not true. There is nothing in that teaching about standards of conduct or moral judgements, there is only the urgent call to recognize the challenge of the proclamation and to respond to it" (Perrin 1967, 109).

It was not Jesus' purpose, then, to bring a new code of ethics into the world, a code that would differ decisively from that of Greek philosophy or Jewish wisdom. The parables of Jesus, the parable of the cross, are not illustrations of "how we should behave," nor are they answers to the moral dilemmas human persons face every day. They are radical challenges to our powers of recognition. By subverting our ordinary expectations about how God works in the world, they force us to reassess all our "codes," all our established systems of behavior and evaluation. That is why the work of conversion never ends. Even when we are ethically "good," "morally upright," conversion challenges our power to recognize and respond to God at work in the unexpected places of human life.

There is an excellent example of this point in a short story entitled "Revelation" by Flannery O'Connor. The story tells of an encounter between a plump respectable Christian lady named Ruby Turpin and an acne-scarred college girl from Wellesley named Mary Grace. The two meet at a doctor's office one summer afternoon in a small southern town —and the meeting becomes an astonishing moment of recognition for Ruby. There was nothing wicked about Ruby Turpin; she was a virtuous woman, conscious of her weaknesses but grateful for the good things life had given her. Her sincere goal in life was to "help anybody who needs it":

> To help anybody out that needed it was her philosophy of
> life. She never spared herself when she found somebody in
> need, whether they were white or black, trash or decent.
> And of all she had to be thankful for, she was most thank-
> ful that this was so (O'Connor 1965, 175).

As she sat in the doctor's office that hot summer afternoon, Mrs. Turpin couldn't help sharing her gratitude—and her philosophy of life—with anyone who would listen. She chattered agreeably about illness and weather, cotton fields and the difficulty of finding reliable hired help. Above all, she testified to her gratitude:

> "If it's one thing I am," Mrs. Turpin said with feeling, "It's
> grateful. When I think who all I could have been besides my-
> self and what all I got, a little of everything, and a good dis-
> position besides, I just feel like shouting, Thank you, Jesus,
> for making everything the way it is!" (O'Connor 1965, 177).

All the while Ruby was chattering, the girl from Wellesley—Mary Grace— was turning purple with rage. Finding Mrs. Turpin's testimony about gratitude too much to bear, she leaped to her feet and began clawing at Ruby's rather considerable bulk of flesh. Caught entirely off-guard, Mrs. Turpin was wounded and stunned. Something about the girl was menacing, familiar: "There was no doubt in her mind that the girl did know her, knew her in some intense and personal way, beyond time and place and condition" (O'Connor 1965, 178). As the ruckus died down, Ruby heard the girl whisper directly to her: "Go back to hell where you came from, you old wart hog" (O'Connor 1965, 179).

After she and her husband had left the doctor's office and returned home to their farm, Mrs. Turpin found herself unable to forget the girl's twisted accusation:

> The girl's eyes and her words, even the tone of her voice,
> low but clear, directed only to her, brooked no repudiation.
> She had been singled out for the message, though there was
> trash in the room to whom it might justly have been applied.
> The full force of this fact struck her . . . There was a woman
> there who was neglecting her own child but she had been over-
> looked. The message had been given to Ruby Turpin, a respect-
> able, hardworking, church-going woman (O'Connor 1965, 180).

Why had *she* been singled out for the "message"? How was she a "wart hog"? As she turned these questions over in her mind, Mrs. Turpin's anger rose until, gazing toward the setting sun, she shouted:

> "If you like trash better, go get yourself some trash then,"
> . . . She shook her fist . . . "I could quit working and take
> it easy and be filthy . . . I could be nasty" . . . A final surge
> of fury shook her and she roared, "Who do you think you
> are?" (O'Connor 1965, 185).

It was at this moment of roaring anger against (God's) "injustice" to her that Ruby Turpin had her moment of revelation, of recognition. For a brief minute the sky seemed to shudder and open, while she witnessed "a vast horde of souls . . . rumbling toward heaven":

> There were whole companies of white-trash, clean for the
> first time in their lives, and . . . battalions of freaks and lun-
> atics shouting and clapping and leaping like frogs. And bring-
> ing up the end of the procession was a tribe of people whom
> she recognized at once as those . . . like herself. . . . Yet she

could see by their shocked and altered faces that even their
virtues were being burned away (O'Connor 1965, 186).

Mrs. Turpin's moment of recognition came in the form of a parable;
and that parable was an acne-pocked college girl named Mary Grace. The
girl's stunning accusation shattered Ruby's own "story" about her life—
a story full of determined virtue and cheerful gratitude. The shock was
subversive, unexpected and profound. Mrs. Turpin learned that even virtue gets burned away, that even the people she despised most (white-
trash, lunatics) were "rumbling toward heaven." Ruby's experience was
similar to what the New Testament calls *metanoia*, conversion or repentance. Caught completely off guard, she recognized that God's sovereign
action was breaking into the world in the most unlikely places.

In the New Testament, therefore, conversion and repentance are not
primarily "ethical." One does not "repent" by substituting one code of
ethics for another. The parables of Jesus are not directly concerned with
norms of behavior or standards for making moral decisions. Repentance
means recognition and response. Through their subversive "twists," the
parables batter down the barriers that prevent our recognizing God's
sovereign activity in the ordinary textures of human life. They reveal that
God's action relativizes all human standards of behavior, that it con-
founds all ordinary expectations about what is good and bad, just and
unjust.

Human Sinfulness and Reconciliation

The view of repentance/conversion (*metanoia*) which we have just
discussed has an important bearing on our understanding of reconciliation
in the New Testament. It is Paul, especially, who sees the salvation and
justification of humanity in terms of God's reconciling activity. In a
well-known passage from the Second Letter to the Corinthians we read:
"It is all God's work. It was God who reconciled us to himself through
Christ and gave us the work of handing on this reconciliation. In other
words, God in Christ was reconciling the world to himself . . . and he
has entrusted to us the news that they are reconciled" (2 Cor. 5:18-19).
This Pauline text, it might be noted, has directly influenced the prayer
of absolution in the new Rite of Penance: "God the Father of mercies,
through the death and resurrection of his Son has *reconciled the world
to himself. . . .* " In order fully to appreciate Paul's view of reconciliation,
it is important to understand how he regarded *unreconciled* humanity,
humanity apart from Christ.

For Paul, unreconciled humanity is *lost, hostile* and *helpless*. There is

an almost flawless description of the Pauline vision of lost humanity in
W.H. Auden's long poetic oratorio, entitled *For the Time Being*:

> Alone, alone, about a dreadful wood
> Of conscious evil runs a lost mankind,
> Dreading to find its Father lest it find
> The Goodness it has dreaded is not good:
> Alone, alone, about our dreadful wood.
> (Auden 1957, 17).

Less poetically but no less accurately, Robin Scroggs has noted that
Paul's view of sinful humanity is characterized by hostility, helplessness
and impotence: *"To be a sinner means to be both helpless and hostile.*
Far from the sinner being a violent person of action, Paul speaks of impotence. . . . Being a sinner is equatable with being unable to achieve
what it is desirable to achieve" (Scroggs 1977, 7). The impotence en-
gendered by human sinfulness is not, in Paul's mind, attached to specific
acts of moral failure or ethical misconduct. Just as Jesus' call to repentance is more radical than any ordinary appeal to ethical standards of
behavior, so Paul's vision of helpless humanity is deeper than personal
error or specific "sins." To Paul's way of thinking, sin is not so much a
matter of doing wrong things; it is a *mode of being.* Scroggs makes this
point forcefully when he writes: " . . . sin is a matter of *existence* which
permeates the total self in all its realities" (Scroggs 1977, 6).

Once again, some of our best modern descriptions of Paul's thought
about impotent sinful humanity come from literature. Flannery O'Connor's work, alluded to earlier, frequently stresses human impotence in
the face of the *real* challenges to action which life offers. In a witty but
somber short story, "The Lame Shall Enter First," O'Connor writes of
Sheppard, a recent widower whose stolid ten-year-old son Norton is a
perpetual disappointment. Sheppard is a good man, committed to liberal
causes and conscious of social issues like racial inequality and the afflic-
tions of the poor. His work with delinquent boys at a reformatory has
made him painfully sensitive to the injustice which breeds violence and
crime. Desperately, Sheppard tries to conceal his utter inability to love
his own child by concentrating his attention on Rufus Johnson, a lame
inmate at the reformatory. Despite his infinite good will and his altru-
istic intentions, however, Sheppard fails as both father to his son and
benefactor to Johnson. At the end of the story Sheppard's good will is
rejected by the lame Johnson, who screams:

> "I lie and steal because I'm good at it! My foot don't have a
> thing to do with it! The lame shall enter first! The halt'll be
> gathered together. When I get ready to be saved, Jesus'll save
> me, not that lying stinking atheist [Sheppard] . . . "
> (O'Connor 1965, 163).

At that moment Sheppard is awakened to the recognition of his real sinfulness and impotency:

> He had stuffed his own emptiness with good works like a
> glutton. He had ignored his own child to feed his vision of
> himself. He saw the clear-eyed Devil, the sounder of hearts,
> leering at him from the eyes of Johnson (O'Connor 1965,
> 164).

But the recognition comes too late. The impotence that prevented Sheppard from loving his child Norton has taken its ghastly toll—for the
father finds his son dangling from the beam of the attic roof: " . . . the
child hung in the jungle of shadows, just below the beam from which
he had launched his flight into space" (O'Connor 1965, 165).

O'Connor's story of a man's grim powerlessness in the face of a child's
need for love is precisely the mode of existence Paul describes as "sin."
Sheppard's "sin" did not consist in high crimes and wicked deeds but in
the crippling impotence which paralyzes a person when loving action is
most required. To repeat Robin Scrogg's phrase: "Being a sinner is equatable with being unable to achieve what it is desirable to achieve" (Scroggs
1977, 7). As a fundamental condition of human existence, sin transcends
mere misbehavior, even when the misbehavior is serious and destructive.
In the most radical sense, what makes human beings sinners are not wicked
deeds; the deeds are merely manifestations of the existential condition
of hostility and helplessness. Our sin has deeper roots—ones that cannot
be eradicated simply by the noble intention to 'do good' and 'avoid
evil.'"

It is this view of human sinfulness that gives substance to Paul's message of reconciliation. For Paul sees the work of God in Christ as above
all a work of reconciling, of restoring a relationship between humanity
and God which was lost through the *power* (hostility, helplessness, impotence) of sin. This act of reconciliation is "all *God's* work" (2 Cor. 5:18).
God did not need to be reconciled or appeased; it is egregiously contrary
to Paul's thinking to suggest that Jesus had to die in order to placate the

13

anger of a God grown hostile and surly toward humanity. As William Barclay has observed: "It was man, not God, who needed to be reconciled. Nothing has lessened the love of God; nothing had turned that love to hate; nothing had ever banished that yearning from the heart of God. . . . It was not God who needed to be pacified, but man who needed to be moved to surrender and to penitence and to love. . . . The effect of the Cross changed, not the heart of God, but the heart of man" (Barclay 1964, 167).

If Jesus' death "reconciles" and "justifies" humanity—and Paul argued that it does—then this happens because the parable of the cross breaks once and for all the paralyzing hostility of the human heart. The power of God meets the powerlessness of the cross—and the result is salvation, freedom for the human person: "When we were reconciled to God by the death of his Son, we were *still enemies*; now that we have been reconciled, surely we may count on being saved by the life of his Son?" (Romans 5:10).

It is important to notice that for Paul *reconciliation* (another name for "justification") does not consist in God's grudging cancellation of this or that wicked deed; it consists, radically, in *liberation,* release from that existential power or condition of sin described earlier as hostility, helplessness and impotence. To borrow a phrase from Gunther Bornkamm, reconciliation in the Pauline sense means "release from sin as a power which makes men its slaves" (Bornkamm 1968, 151).

Paul's thinking about "God at work in Christ" has some significant implications for our own theology of reconciliation. First, Paul does *not* regard reconciliation as either, (1) the human effort to placate God's hostility toward people (this, indeed, would be a manifestation of *sin*—the effort to justify oneself before God, even by pious works), or (2) God's cancellation of a specific list of human crimes and misdemeanors. God's act of reconciling the world in Christ was not an "absolution" imparted after a sufficient number of penitents had confessed their sins according to number, species and circumstances. Secondly, just as Paul regarded sin as a *mode of existence,* so also he acknowledged reconciliation as an *enduring* existential fact. Reconciliation is not a temporary reprieve bestowed on humanity by a sly God who secretly plans to drop the other shoe when we least expect it. The good news of reconciliation is not that God's seething anger has been temporarily calmed or averted, but that human rebellion has been transformed into surrender. That transformation has been wrought by the parable of the cross. For the cross is at once the ultimate "acting out" of human rebellion and the definitive surrender of humanity to the heart of God. "The language of the cross may be illogical to those who are not on the way to salvation," Paul wrote to the Corinthians, "but those of us who are on the way see it as God's power to save" (1 Cor. 1:17).

Message and Sacrament

The New Testament theology of cross, conversion and reconciliation has some important ramifications for sacramental practice in the church today. In popular catechesis and pastoral practice the sacrament of penance has frequently been presented as something *we* do for God. The humiliation of sin, failure and guilt, the difficulty of confessing one's sins to another human being, the necessary sentiments of contrition and sorrow: these, it has been said, are the "sacrifices" we bring to God when we seek forgiveness and pardon. The sacrament has been regarded as a "work," a humiliating task that must be endured if we are to have assurance that God's mercy will triumph over punishment. According to this point of view, reconciliation is a kind of bilateral peace treaty: *we* promise to confess, admit our guilt and accept a penance; *God,* for his part, promises to bestow forgiveness, provided the treaty's conditions have been sincerely fulfilled. Reconciliation becomes a negotiated contract that results from *our* willingness to confess sins and do penance, and from *God's willingness* either to "look the other way" or to mitigate his justifiable displeasure. The sacrament of penance becomes an opportunity to *earn* God's friendship once more by a faithful performance of confession, contrition and self-denial.

These contract theories of the sacrament have relatively little to do with the New Testament's message of repentance (*metanoia*) and reconciliation. Indeed, such theories are opposed to the Pauline theology of God's reconciling activity in Christ. For the attempt to *earn* salvation is precisely what Paul regards as *sin* and *disobedience* in the most radical sense of those terms. As we have seen, Paul views sin primarily as sinful existence, "an existence which contains within it qualities of impotence and hostility toward God *even in the moment of perfect fulfillment of the law*" (Scroggs, 1977, 8). According to Pauline thought, the effort to establish a contract or to negotiate a peace treaty with God is disobedience. Robin Scroggs writes: " . . . disobedience consists in the attempt to establish one's own justification—to understand one's life as a project to win and secure one's existence. . . . By attending to this project I attempt to ease the anxiety about my own security" (Scroggs 1977, 8).

15

One is reminded here of the figure of Ruby Turpin, the cheerful, hard-working, church-going lady in Flannery O'Connor's short story "Revelation." The idea that she, rather than some detestable "white trash," has been singled out for the scalding "message" outraged Mrs. Turpin.

> "Why me?" she rumbled. "It's no trash around here, black
> or white, that I haven't given to. And break my back to the
> bone every day working. And do for the church" (O'Connor
> 1965, 184).

As we have seen, revelation happens for Mrs. Turpin when she finally realizes that "even virtue gets burned away" in the astonishing presence of God. A similar moment of truth occurs for Sheppard in the story "The Lame Shall Enter First." Sheppard is jolted (too late) out of his unloving impotence when he recognizes that he has "stuffed his own emptiness with good works like a glutton" and has "ignored his own child to feed his vision of himself" (O'Connor 1965, 164).

Both Ruby Turpin and Sheppard are examples of "disobedience" in the Pauline sense of the word. Their very effort to "be good" and their very devotion to "virtue" has made them unloving, helpless people. Both of them have *used* people in an effort to overcome anxiety about their own "salvation." Mrs. Turpin likes blacks only because they give her a chance to prove how kind a white lady can be. Sheppard helps Rufus Johnson only because he affords him the opportunity of revealing his dedication to the causes of poverty and injustice. Reconciliation happens for Mrs. Turpin and for Sheppard only when a "vision" destroys their scrupulously planned virtue. For Ruby Turpin the vision takes the form of "lunatics and white trash" rumbling into heaven; for Sheppard the vision assumes the more tragic dimension of a child dangling from the beam of an attic. In both cases, reconciliation happens when disobedience (the effort to secure and justify one's own existence) has been overcome by an utterly unexpected recognition of God at work in a very human world.

These examples help to show that reconciliation in the New Testament sense does not consist in plea-bargaining with God. Nor does it have anything to do with amassing virtue so that God will somehow be forced, in justice, to bestow grace and salvation. If the radical meaning of repentance is "recognition and response," then the meaning of reconciliation is *obedience* and *surrender.* Being obedient to the word of the gospel does not mean the perfect fulfilling of laws, regulations and prescriptions.

It means, instead, letting go, giving up our pretentious claims to goodness and holiness, surrendering to the power of God's love that burns even our virtues away.

It is this subversive love of God that the sacrament of reconciliation intends to celebrate. The sacrament is important not because it *removes* something (sin, guilt, punishment), but because it *proclaims* something: that God reconciles us precisely as enemies, precisely as sinners (cf. Romans 5:10). While one would not want to repudiate the psychological benefits of confession (the alleviation of anxiety through the disclosure of failure and guilt to another person), such benefits are not the primary purpose of reconciliation as a sacramental celebration of the church's faith. The fundamental intention of the sacrament is not the excavation of the human psyche nor even the therapeutic release of anxiety. The sacrament of reconciliation is a proclamation of faith; it is a public moment of thanksgiving and praise when the church confesses its faith in the God whose predictable love appears in unpredictable places.

Like the stories of Jesus and like the cross itself, the sacrament of reconciliation is a parable. Its message is provocative, subversive, unexpected; it overturns all human judgements about virtue and vice, sinners and saints. As a parable the sacrament of reconciliation continues the proclamation of the kingdom begun in the ministry of Jesus. Jesus announced a kingdom where the great are small, the rich are poor, the lepers are clean, the prostitutes are virtuous, the sinners sit down at table with God, and the mighty cedars of Lebanon are scrubby mustard plants. This kingdom, Jesus suggested, defies all human expectations about how God works in the world. To the powerful, God's reign will appear shabby, incompetent and absurd; to the powerless, it will appear awesome, royal and overwhelming. To *all,* God's reign will be puzzling, controversial and even annoying. Predictions about it are useless—it comes like a thief in the night; theologies about it are futile—its secret is revealed to the unlearned.

The sacrament of reconciliation is a parable of this reign or kingdom of God. Far from being an occasion of private surgery where sins are aborted in secret, reconciliation publicly announces the central paradox of Christian faith: the fact that the words "God," "love" and "sinner" must be put together in the same sentence. W.H. Auden has captured this paradoxical sense of sinful humanity in the presence of God's love in the following lines from his poem *For the Time Being*:

17

> The Inevitable is what will seem to happen to you purely
>   by chance;
> The Real is what will strike you as really absurd;
> Unless you are certain you are dreaming, it is certainly a
>   dream of your own;
> Unless you exclaim—"There must be some mistake"—you
>   must be mistaken. (Auden 1957, 18)

The ministry of reconciliation is, then, part of that larger ministry of the *Word* which Paul claimed to serve. There is nothing clinical about sacramental reconciliation; it is not a dispensary where divine medicines are exchanged for human illnesses. The word of forgiveness responds to the ineradicable human longing for *freedom*. To repent means to recognize and respond; to reconcile means to release and restore. God's act of reconciliation in Christ does not merely absolve sins, it frees persons from the sinful mode of existence that makes them slaves to hostility and helplessness. It liberates people not only from failure and guilt but also from the suffocating goodness and virtue through which we attempt to earn salvation. The gospel of forgiveness is God's ultimate word of freedom uttered in the face of humanity's frantic effort to justify itself.

This gospel is proclaimed to the Christian most radically in baptism, the fundamental sacrament of freedom and restoration. It is proclaimed repeatedly in the eucharist, where sinners sit at table while they joyfully await the full disclosure of God's reign. And it is proclaimed in the sacrament of reconciliation where the church gives thanks (makes eucharist) in still another way by acknowledging God's subversive power at work in the parable of the cross. For in the cross we recognize the ultimate sign of human rebellion and failure transformed into the sign of pardon and peace. Because it proclaims the parable of the cross, the sacrament of reconciliation can take both sin and grace with full seriousness. Personal sins *are* serious; they are a concrete acting out of that asphixiating hostility that makes us empty and impotent when we are challenged to love. But grace is serious, too. For grace is God acting out in us, God giving us his own name: freedom.

Thus, when the new Rite of Penance instructs ministers of the sacrament to welcome penitents warmly and joyfully, it is not simply repeating weary sentiments of benevolence and good will. For in the sacrament of reconciliation penitents themselves become parables, stories that subvert our ordinary expectations about the way God acts in human lives. As parables, sinners are "something human," something scarred, worn and loved by God. Only people who know the story of sin can share Paul's astonished cry: "Death, where is your victory? Death, where is your sting? Now the sting of death is sin, and sin gets its power from the Law. So let us thank God for giving us the victory through our Lord Jesus Christ" (1 Cor. 15:55-57).

References

Auden, W.H., "For the Time Being," in *Religious Drama, I: Five Plays.* New York: World Publishing Co., 1957.

Barclay, William. *New Testament Words.* London: SCM Press, 1964.

Bornkamm, Gunther. *Paul.* Translated by D.M.G. Stalker, New York: Harper and Row, 1971.

Crossan, John Dominic. *The Dark Interval.* Niles, Illinois: Argus Communications, 1975.

O'Connor, Flannery. *Everything That Rises Must Converge.* New York: New York: New American Library, 1965.

Perrin, Norman. *Rediscovering the Teaching of Jesus.* New York: Harper and Row, 1967.

Scroggs, Robin. *Paul for a New Day.* Philadelphia: Fortress Press, 1977.

Tolkien, J.R.R. *The Tolkien Reader.* New York: Ballantine Books, 1966.

Wicker, Brian. *The Story-Shaped World.* Notre Dame, Indiana: University of Notre Dame Press, 1975.

Wigginton, Eliot, ed. *The Foxfire Book.* New York: Doubleday Anchor Books, 1972.

Winter, Paul, "Sadducees and Pharisees," in *Jesus in His Time.* Edited by Hans Jurgen Schultz. Philadelphia: Fortress Press, 1971.

CHAPTER TWO

The Many Ways to Reconciliation: An Historical Synopsis of Christian Penance

Nathan Mitchell, OSB

About fifteen years ago Walter M. Miller published a popular science-fiction novel entitled *Canticle for Leibowitz*. Miller's *Canticle* is not an immortal contribution to English prose, but it does tell an intriguing and even plausible story. In this novel, the world has been devastated by nuclear holocaust and an eerie "age of simplification" has followed. Books and literature—especially those that deal with technological engineering and weaponry—have been banished from the earth. Reading has become an uncommon art pursued only in remote places like monasteries. At one of these monasteries, located in what remains of the American Southwest, some scientific documents from an earlier age have been preserved. None of the monks, however, is capable of deciphering the complicated mathematical symbols, chemical formulas and physical laws that these documents conceal. As time passes, the age of simplification wanes and technology returns once more. The *Canticle* describes the rapid rediscovery of weapons and warfare and concludes with a second apocalyptic scene of nuclear destruction.

There are times when every person who works in liturgical planning and celebration must surely long for an age of simplification. The world of worship today is littered with study papers, guidelines, memoranda, manuals of celebration, policy statements and episcopal admonitions. It is easy to lose oneself in a cloud of paper and ink and to forget what even so dedicated an academician as Thomas Aquinas remembered: sacraments are for *people*. When all is said and done, liturgy's most basic resources are the raw stuff of human lives, the rag-tag textures of human experience. Ultimately, liturgists have to do what poets do: they have to listen attentively to the speech of ordinary people and then shape that speech into songs people can recognize as their own—songs about finding and losing, loving and hating, laughing and grieving.

Good poets acknowledge that they are not the first persons who have ever experienced the shock and thunder of human life. People work with language, and language is the common heritage of many generations: it has a history. Like language, liturgy also has a history. Christians did not invent worship any more than they invented eating, drinking or dancing. Nor did Christians invent serious human issues like failure and guilt, sin and repentance. Some of humanity's earliest recorded literature speaks of hope for god-like mercy in the face of failure. An ancient Egyptian psalm, for example, written down about 1300 B.C., exclaims: "The servant was bent on doing wrong; yet the Lord (Amun) was bent on being merciful" (Thomas 1961, 153). The struggle to find forgiveness is an ancient one, rooted deeply in human consciousness.

This struggle was no stranger to the people of Israel and to the earliest Christians. Israel wrestled with Yahweh, the God of the covenant, the Lord who offered his people a choice between life and blessing, or death and disaster: "I call heaven and earth to witness against you today: I set before you life or death, blessing or curse. Choose life, then, so that you and your descendants may live, in the love of Yahweh your God, obeying his voice, clinging to him; for in this your life consists" (Deuteronomy 30:19-20). And Jesus, the pathfinder of a new covenant, wrestled with the will of his Father in a garden and on a cross: "You were dead, because you were sinners and had not been circumcised: he has brought you to life with him, he has forgiven us all our sins. He has overidden the Law, and cancelled every record of the debt that we had to pay; he has done away with it by nailing it to the cross" (Colossians 2:13-14).

The earliest Christians were convinced that Jesus' struggle with sin and death on the cross had resulted in liberation for believers. In the sixth chapter of the Letter to the Romans, Paul argued eloquently that baptism means plunging into Jesus' death—and that Jesus' death means liberation from the slavery of sin: " . . . When we were baptised in Christ Jesus we were baptised in his death . . . so that as Christ was raised from the dead by the Father's glory, we too might live a new life. . . . We must realise that our former selves have been crucified with him . . . to free us from the slavery of sin. When a man dies, of course, he has finished with sin" (Romans 6:3-7).

This radical liberation from sin did not, however, free Christians from the struggle against failure, impotent selfishness and personal irresponsibility. A swift glance at Paul's letters to the community at Corinth will show that Christians continued to wrestle with evil and failure even after their baptismal death to sin. As time went on, believers became even more intensely conscious of a paradox at the heart of their experience of faith: Christians were both saved and sinful, liberated from sin's hostile power yet haunted by a continuing need for repentance. If repentance, faith and baptism mean death to sin, was it possible for Christians who "fell" after baptism to remain members of the community? Was a "second repentance" after baptism possible? Or was a sinful baptized Christian utterly cut off from the community without hope of return?

These questions were not speculative ones debated by early Christians scholars as exercises in logic. They were practical issues that demanded the immediate pastoral attention of the whole Christian community. On the one hand, sin seemed incompatible with a community that regarded itself as thoroughly cleansed, without "spot or wrinkles," "holy and faultless" (see Ephesians 5:27). On the other hand, sin continued to reveal itself in the lives of Christian communities, through incest at Corinth (1 Cor. 5), through disunity (James 4), through wrangling and jealousy (Gal. 5:19-20). Pastorally speaking, how were Christians to deal with members whose lives challenged the integrity of the community's love and belief? Should the community forgive and forget? reject and punish? hope and pray for the sinner's return?

These pastoral questions had to be resolved by a community which wa was often regarded by "outsiders" with suspicion and hostility. For the early Christian church not only claimed to *believe* certain things, it also claimed that these beliefs had direct and immediate repercussions on the way people live in the world. "Right faith" (orthodoxy) was inseparable from "right action" (orthopraxy). Belief and behavior were the sides of a single coin. To paraphrase Paul, "dead people don't sin" (Romans 6:7). Sin in the Christian community not only damaged its public image as a "consecrated nation" of persons who had died in baptism (1 Peter 2:9); it also threatened the integrity of faith itself. Sin was a form of denial, a shattering repudiation of the knowledge of God born of faith: "Anyone who sins has never seen God nor known him" (1 John 3:6). Thus the problem of sin after baptism raised a serious question about the very nature of Christian faith itself. How could God's holy people, washed in Jesus' blood, permit sinners to continue in their midst? Pastoral problems like these could not be resolved overnight. They demanded reflection, experimentation, practical experience and sensitive attention. In the pages that follow we will examine some of the critical decisions reached by the Christian community in its efforts to deal with the pastoral problem of sin. Our examination will not provide a complete history of the sacrament of penance through the ages, but it will suggest some of the ways Christians have dealt with the presence of sin in the baptized community.

Rigor and Realism: Christian Penance in the First Three Centuries

The development of penance in the baptized community has been described and debated by a number of scholars in the twentieth century. Since not all writers agree about the evidence for penance in the ancient church, it may be useful to outline two common theories about this evidence.

Theory 1: Rigor and Laxity. Some writers have tried to trace the history of Christian penance by observing that the earliest attitude toward sinners in the community was one of uncompromising rigor. This view asserts that Christians originally opposed the notion that penance for sin after baptism was effective but that as laxity and moral laziness entered the church's life, some provision had to be made for baptized people who failed. The theory implies that the original Christian position was supremely rigorous: no second chances after baptism; no compromises with sinners who lost their "baptismal innocence." Since baptism meant new creation and new life, no amount of community intercession or personal conversion would repair the damage wrought by serious infidelity after baptism. To sin after "being washed" was to forfeit one's membership in the community of faith. The sinner had to be removed, thrown on the mysterious mercy of God; the community itself was helpless to restore the unfortunate member to the life of faith and worship.

This theory continued by arguing that, as Christianity spread and its initial fervor waned, pressure increased to find a more satisfactory solution for the problem of those who sinned after baptism. Unhappily and reluctantly, the church was forced to admit that the ideal of a sinless life was more often recognized in the breach than in the fulfillment. And so, this theory maintains, a process was established that would gradually restore the sinner to communion with the church after a prolonged period of prayer, penance, fasting and good works.

Theory 2: Pastoral Realism. More recently, scholars have begun to challenge the assumption that the early church was uncompromising and utterly rigorous in its attitude toward post-baptismal sinners. Unquestionably there were some Christian communities which stressed the utter incompatibility between sinners and the "saved community." But even in the early Christian documents that speak of penance for the baptized, there is a strong dose of pastoral realism. The idea of sinlessness is upheld, but it is tempered by compassion for the weakness of members who, like Paul, experienced "a different law that battles against the law which reason dictates" (Romans 7:23). This second theory suggests, then, that the early Christian church's attitude toward sin was neither rigorous nor lax but pastorally realistic. The church could not simply abandon sinners and leave them without hope of repentance or return to the community. Some process had to be established that would permit the community to uphold its ideal of sinlessness and, at the same time, hold out hope to members who failed to meet the gospel's call to a blameless life.

This second theory seems better suited to the evidence we possess from the earliest centuries of Christianity. We have, for example, an early document known as *The Shepherd of Hermas* that comes from the church at Rome around the middle of the second century (perhaps about A.D. 140) Interpretations of this document vary, but the most plausible one suggests that the author of *The Shepherd* was trying to steer a middle course between rigorous intransigence on the one hand and free-wheeling laxity on the other. Thus, *The Shepherd* recognizes that penance is available to the baptized sinner, that reconciliation with God and the community is *possible,* but that such an opportunity is *limited.* The author speaks of a "jubilee period" of God's mercy that invites baptized sinners to do penance and seek reconciliation with the church. This jubilee of mercy is extended *only* to people who have been Christians for a long while; it is not available to men and women who are just entering the way of conversion (catechumens) or who have just been baptized (neophytes). *The Shepherd,* then, argues that mercy, repentance and return are possible for baptized sinners who sincerely do penance.

Another early Christian document known as the *First Letter of Clement* (from about A.D. 96) also hints that penance for the baptized sinner is possible. Actually a letter written by the Christian community at Rome to the church at Corinth, *First Clement,* emphasizes the role of the community's prayer and intercession on behalf of those who need repentance. The sinner is not to be utterly ignored and abandoned; he is to be offered help and healing through the intercession and prayer of other Christians. This is an important point because it shows that the power of reconciliation *resides in the entire community of believers. All* Christians have a part to play in calling the sinner back to faith and communion.

Admittedly, these early references to penance are often fragmentary, incomplete. They stem from a period of time when the church's structures of ministry and discipline were still rather fluid and flexible. We cannot use documents like *The Shepherd of Hermas* or *First Clement* to "prove" that a fully-developed system of sacramental penance existed in the early church. Nor can we use these documents to deny that penance was available to baptized sinners. We can see in them, however, a growing realism about the pastoral response to sin and the sinner. They reflect the church's concern for finding a way to welcome sinners back into the full communion of faith and worship. It is reasonably accurate, then, to say that some of our earliest Christian literature stresses penance as an opportunity for the sinner's reintegration into the community. Indeed, the early church seems to have recoiled from the idea that a sinner might be abandoned without any hope of repentance and return.

During the second and third centuries, the Fathers of the Church also struggled with the pastoral issue of sin. The wrestling was particularly prominent in the church of North Africa, where men like Tertullian (ca. A.D. 160-225) and St. Cyprian of Carthage (died in A.D. 258) were at work. Each of these men contributed significantly to the discussion about sin and penance in the Christian community. Tertullian, a passionate but sour apologist for the faith, was strongly committed to a view of Christianity which stressed discipline and ascetical rigor. After his conversion (sometime before A.D. 197), he used his considerable skill as a rhetorician in the defense of Christian doctrine. Tertullian was especially vigorous in maintaining the true humanity of Jesus against those heretics who denied that the Lord shared fully the condition of human flesh. He also wrote an important work on Christian baptism, one of the earliest treatises on that subject that we possess.

At the same time, however, Tertullian was a man intensely suspicious of anything that smacked of laxity in the Christian church. In about A.D. 207, his rigorism drove him to join the Montanists, a sect that emphasized the immediate presence of the Spirit in Christian prophets, as well as a staunch program of asceticism leading to moral perfection. As both a Christian and a Montanist, Tertullian wrote works on the subject of sin and penance. In his short book, *On Penance,* written while he was still a Christian in good standing, Tertullian spoke of a *second* penance available to people who sinned after baptism (baptism itself being the first penance). According to Tertullian, this second penance was literally a once-in-a-lifetime opportunity. Appealing to a nautical metaphor, he described penance as "a second plank thrown to the (drowning sinner) after shipwreck." He also warned against using this unique opportunity for mercy as an excuse for frequent sinning. Tertullian also furnishes us with a glimpse of the pastoral procedures used for penance in the North African church of his day. First, he speaks of the sinner's *admission of guilt* (probably communicated privately to the bishop or to a presbyter); following this admission the sinner wept, prayed, fasted. Tertullian's advice was: "The less you spare yourself, the more God will spare you!" Secondly, the penitent sought the *intercession of the whole* community gathered for prayer. When the period of penance was completed, the sinner was reconciled to the community by the bishop.

25

After his conversion to the Montanist sect, however, Tertullian's latent rigorism became explicit and even nasty. He contended that some sins were, quite simply, unforgivable. No amount of prayer and intercession could remit what Tertullian called *peccata capitalia* (literally, capital sins). In his work *On Modesty (De Pudicitia),* Tertullian complained bitterly about bishops who had the audacity to reconcile Christians guilty of sins (capital sins) like adultery and fornication. He heaped abuse on such pastors, calling them sarcastic names like "big chief bridge-builders" and "super-bishops." Actually, Tertullian's distinction between "forgivable" and "unforgivable" sins was rather innovative, because the rest of the Christian church tended to regard *all* sins as forgivable so long as persons were sincerely willing to seek repentance. Even if sinners were required to do penance until they reached their deathbeds, reconciliation was still to be granted them. But Tertullian the Montanist denied this principle and argued that people guilty of capital sins (murder, adultery, fraud, idolatry) should never be reconciled. God's mercy alone could save them.

Most Christians found Tertullian's gloomy approach to penance unacceptable. They concluded that God's mercy was offered to sinners through the prayer, intercession and ministry of the church. But this conclusion was not reached without controversy. For example, in the middle of the third century, St. Cyprian, bishop of Carthage in North Africa, was forced to deal with a pastoral situation that had developed as a result of persecution launched against Christians by the Roman emperor Decius. Some believers had collapsed under the pressure of this persecution; they apostasized and offered sacrifice to the Roman gods. Those who had repudiated their faith in this way were called "the lapsed," and it was Cyprian's job as bishop to discover a way these men and women could be brought back into the community once the persecution had ended. As a pastor, Cyprian felt it was *his* responsibility to decide how and when the lapsed were to be reconciled.

In the course of deciding this matter, however, Cyprian found himself embroiled in controversy on two different fronts. In his own church at Carthage he came into conflict with a practice known as the "martyrs' privilege." These martyrs were not people who had actually died, but men and women who had suffered for their faith and were consequently regarded as heroic persons in the community. Sometimes, indeed, these martyrs were given the rank of presbyter without any formal ordination by the bishop. Cyprian's position was that a lengthy period of penance should be an indispensable condition for reconciliation with the church. The martyrs, who also claimed the right to reconcile penitents, were much more swift about granting pardon and restoration to the lapsed.

Cyprian found himself caught between his own vision of a bishop's responsibilities and the martyrs' popular claim to the right of granting pardon and peace to sinners. Eventually, Cyprian's position carried the day —and it marked an important step in the establishment of *episcopal control* over the process of penance and reconciliation in the church.

On another front, Cyprian became involved in a quarrel with Stephen, the bishop of Rome (about 254). The immediate occasion of this dispute was not the discipline of penance but the legitimacy of baptism administered by heretical persons. Arguing on the principle that one who does not possess the Spirit cannot bestow it in sacramental celebrations, Cyprian denied the validity of baptism given by heretics (i.e., by people who had "lost" the Spirit by damaging the unity of the church). Arguing on a contrary principle—that the effectiveness of a sacrament is not determined by the personal qualities of the minister—Bishop Stephen upheld the legitimacy of baptism by heretics. At issue in this quarrel was a very important matter, one that still affects us today: Is a sacrament effective because of the minister's personal faith and holiness—or it is effective because God freely offers and gives himself in grace even when ministers are corrupt and inept?

On this front Cyprian was less successful; it was Stephen's view that eventually prevailed. Both of Cyprian's controversies, with the martyrs and with Bishop Stephen, are significant for the history of penance. The first (dealing with the "martyrs' privilege") contributed to the view, strong in the Western churches, that the *bishop* has primary responsibility for the process of penance and reconciliation among his people. The second (Cyprian's quarrel with Stephen) contributed to a commonplace principle in the theology of the sacraments: the sacraments are understood to be effective in virtue of God's power at work in Christ, not in virtue of the personal merits of a minister.

By the latter part of the third century, then, the Christian community had already made some strategic pastoral decisions about sin and sinners in the church. We may summarize these decisions as follows:

1. There was a growing consensus that penance after baptism is possible *at least once* in a person's lifetime. Furthermore, *all* sins are forgivable, even ones (like murder or apostasy) that seriously compromise the community's life and faith.

2. There was a growing recognition of the centrality of the *bishop's* role in the work of reconciliation. As shepherd and healer among his people, the bishop was held responsible for promoting an environment where sinners could find a welcome back into the community, provided they were sincere in their search for conversion and repentance.

3. In contrast to the rigor of people like Tertullian, most Christians sought to deal with baptized sinners in a way that combined pastoral realism and compassion. The idea of utterly abandoning sinners and refusing to welcome them back seems to have been repulsive to most orthodox writers of this period.

4. The position that sacraments are effective despite the personal worthiness of ministers began to gain wide, though not universal, acceptance.

Public Penance: The Fourth through the Sixth Centuries

We have already seen that the early centuries of Christian life reveal the growth of pastoral realism, as opposed to inflexible rigor, in handling the issue of sin in the baptized community. The most significant development in the next historical period, from the fourth through the sixth centuries, is the emergence of what is ordinarily called "public penance" or "public canonical penance." These terms refer to that ensemble of liturgical rites and penitential practices required of Christians who were guilty of serious infidelity. This public discipline involved several steps, which may be outlined here.

1. *"Seeking penance"*. The baptized Christian who was guilty of serious and public sin was expected to admit his guilt before the bishop or his representative (usually a presbyter). This confession was probably made in private, even when the sin committed was widely known in the community. Occasionally the sinner may have been denounced by the bishop and charged with the responsibility of seeking penance.

2. *Enrolling in the "order of penitents"*. Once the sinner had revealed his guilt to the bishop, he was formally excommunicated and enrolled in the "order of penitents." This meant that the person was disbarred from full participation in the community's eucharist (penitents were asked to leave after the liturgy of the Word).

3. *Doing works of penance.* The penitents were required to fast, to pray and, sometimes, to dress in rough clothing of sackcloth. The period of penance was customarily determined by the bishop. Its length could amount to several years, depending upon the gravity of the offense and the sinner's previous status in the community (e.g., bishops, presbyters and deacons were required to do penance for longer periods and were usually stripped of their ecclesiastical rank).

28

4. *Reconciling.* Upon completion of the assigned period of penance, penitents were formally reconciled and restored to the eucharistic fellowship of the community. As time went on, it became customary to perform this rite of reconciliation for penitents on Holy Thursday. Some of our ancient liturgical books provide rites and prayers for this purpose, though it is difficult to know how frequently they were actually used. The bishop presided over the rite of reconciliation, imposed hands on the penitents as a sign of their restoration to the community of faith, and prayed for their forgiveness and healing. A sample of the type of prayer used in this rite of reconciliation may be found in a document known as the *Gelasian Sacramentary,* a book of Roman and French liturgical material that circulated widely in Europe during the eighth century. The bishop prays: "O God, you purify the hearts of those who confess to you and you free burdened consciences from every bond of evil. Grant forgiveness to sinners and healing to the wounded. May those who have received forgiveness of all their sins serve you steadfastly with sincere devotion—and may they never lose your eternal salvation: through Christ our Lord."

Even after their reconciliation, however, some stigma still remained with those who had done public penance. They were, for example, forbidden to serve as ministers in the community, and married persons were expected to abstain from intercourse with their spouses.

During this historical period two practical rules of thumb seem to have emerged as ways to handle the pastoral problem of sin in the community. One such rule is often called the "rule of a single penance." This meant that Christians could seek public penance *only once* in a lifetime. Backsliders could not count on being given the opportunity to do penance a second time (though it was customary to reconcile such people on their deathbeds). The second rule of thumb was this: *public* penance is required in cases of infidelity that are public and scandalous; a *private* program of penance (fasting, charitable works—not private confession) is expected of Christians guilty of private or interior sins. There were, of course, some exceptions to these rules of thumb. For example, St. Ambrose, bishop of Milan (about 339-397), seems to have expected his people to do penance publicly even for "secret sins."

From this brief description it can be seen that public penance was often a grim and arduous affair. For all practical purposes, becoming a penitent was like becoming a monk. Since penitents were usually required to assume a celibate lifestyle, their marriages were severely altered. And since penitents were also expected to spend long hours in fasting, prayer and works of charity, it would have been difficult for them to hold down an ordinary job. Public penance thus implied drastic changes in the marital and economic condition of Christian penitents.

The pastoral impracticality of public canonical penance led some bishops, like Caesarius of Arles (about 470-552), to encourage their people to *avoid* seeking admission into the order of penitents unless they were well on in years (over fifty years of age), seriously ill, or at the point of death. In place of the discipline associated with public penance, Caesarius encouraged his people to seek forgiveness through prayer, fasting or works of charity and mercy like visiting the sick and the imprisoned. Caesarius and other bishops like him were aware that the severity of public penance and its "once in a lifetime" character were pastorally unrealistic. They sought practical alternatives to public penance because they recognized that while its purposes may have been praiseworthy, it was an all but impossible burden for Christians who had ordinary responsibilities of marriage, family and work.

As a result of the severity of public penance—and of recommendations like those made by Caesarius and others—the formal procedures of public penance were used less and less frequently. Reconciliation for sinners often became a deathbed phenomenon. Since many Christians found the demands of public penance intolerable, they waited until their last illness to seek official reconciliation with the church. During the fourth through the sixth centuries, this sort of deathbed reconciliation did not mean that a priest came rushing to the sickroom to hear the person's confession and give absolution. Sometimes, indeed, if the ill person was at the very point of death, reconciliation was accomplished by administering viaticum, the sacrament of the Lord's body and blood. For at this period in the church's history the sacrament of the dying was neither confession nor extreme unction but the *eucharist,* the sign of the Christian's fellowship with the baptized community. Even if the sick person was not at the very point of death, he or she was reconciled not by confession and absolution but by that ancient sacramental gesture of healing and restoration —the imposition of hands.

It is also important to notice that during these centuries theologians and pastorally minded bishops like St. Augustine (354-430) debated the effectiveness of penance done by baptized Christians who had sinned. Augustine, for example, emphasized the notion that sinners are reconciled with God precisely by being reconciled with the Christian community. Peace and communion with the church brings the Spirit's peace to the sinner. In his preaching and pastoral catechesis, Augustine used the story of Lazarus from John's gospel to explain his point about the importance of reconciliation with the Christian community. The sinner,

Augustine noted, is like Lazarus coming forth from the tomb: he is alive once more but he remains bound until he has been fully restored to communion through the church's ministry. For Augustine, both the performance of penitential works and official reconciliation through the church's ministry are necessary if the sinner is to find peace and pardon. While Christians were not expected to do public penance for daily sins (less serious failures), Augustine did insist on the public discipline for at least three categories of sin: those of sexual irresponsibility, idolatry (apostasy) and murder.

Augustine's views about the effectiveness of Christian penance also reveal that during this historical period reconciliation was regarded not as a brief magic moment, but as a *process* which requires time, hard work and genuine help and concern from the church's ministers. During the fourth century especially, a number of parallels emerged between the process of Christian initiation and the process of public penance. The following chart shows some of these similarities:

Initiation	*Public Penance*
Enrolling in the catechumenate (period of preparation for baptism: up to three years)	Enrolling in the "order of penitents"
Learning the Christian way through works of conversion and charity	Seeking reconciliation through fasting, works of mercy and charity
Baptismal washing, anointing and imposition of hands as signs of incorporation into the community	Imposition of hands as a sign of peace and communion with the church
Bishop presides at initiation	Bishop presides at reconciliation
A "one time" event	A "one time" event

Such similarities between initiation and public penance led St. Ambrose to comment that "just as there is *one* baptism, so there is *one* public penance."

This historical period roughly between A.D. 300 and 600 represents, therefore, a critically important time in the evolution of Christian penance. It may help to summarize some of the strategic pastoral and theological developments of the period:

1. Public penance underwent noticeable developments which paralleled the procedures for Christian initiation. Those who sinned in ways that were serious, public and scandalous were expected to admit their guilt, enroll themselves in the order of penitents, do works of penance for a considerable length of time (determined by the bishop), abstain from eucharistic fellowship, and finally be reconciled through the ministry of prayer and the imposition of hands.

2. The severity of public penance had begun to produce two results: a) some Christians postponed penance until serious illness, old age or deathbed recommended their requesting it, b) some pastors encouraged their people to seek *alternatives* to public penance like fasting, prayer and works of mercy.

3. Theologians like St. Augustine had begun to emphasize the intimate relation between personal peace with God and public reconciliation with the church. In his view, the grace of reconciliation is *social*; it must be sought in and through the community of faith.

4. Public penance, like baptism, was not repeatable. It was a "one time" event and should not, therefore, be approached recklessly.

The Emergence of "Private Penance": the Seventh Century and After

Quite clearly, the discipline of public penance presented serious pastoral difficulties. Its rigor frightened Christians away and its "once for all" character produced a real impasse for persons who failed frequently. It seems probable that by around A.D. 600, public canonical penance had declined almost to the point of extinction. A growing crisis faced both people and pastors: how could the community maintain its moral standards and, at the same time, offer sinners an opportunity for reconciliation based on a realistic program of repentance and conversion?

This question was not a new one. We have already noticed a similar crisis over the question of penance in our discussion of "rigor versus realism." But by the seventh century some dramatic changes had occurred in the life of the church in Europe that made this crisis more difficult to settle on the pastoral level. During the fifth and sixth centuries, for example, large groups of people were received into the Christian community without much preliminary instruction and catechesis. Perhaps the most memorable example of this phenomenon is the baptism of Clovis (ca. 466-511), King of the Franks. Many of Clovis' tribesmen "followed the leader" and were likewise initiated into Christianity. Baptisms of this sort had enormous *political* repercussions. Membership in the church and membership in civil society were so closely identified that being a Christian and being a citizen became practically synonymous.

There were changes, too, in the baptismal policy of the church. During the sixth century it became more and more customary to baptize persons in infancy. Infants had probably been baptized from the earliest days of Christianity, but for several centuries the pastoral norm for initiating new members had been adult faith and conversion. Now this situation was changing. The common pastoral norm shifted away from adult conversion and initiation toward the baptism of small children.

Such changes in European political structure and sacramental practice had a definite impact on penance in the Christian community. It is one thing to require public penance for men and women who were baptized as adults but it is quite another to require such penance for people who were baptized in infancy and who still have to struggle with all the stages of growth which precede adult maturity. Thus, changes in the church's baptismal policy (the normative shift from adults to children) necessarily affected the process of penance and reconciliation in the community.

It is not surprising, then, that during the seventh century especially, a new form of penance began to appear on the European continent. Scholars today often refer to this new form as "private" or "tariff" penance. The term "tariff" alludes to the practice of assigning specific penances to persons who privately confessed their sins to a priest. These penances were collected in handbooks for confessors known as *Penitential Books (Libri Poenitentiales)*. In such *Penitential Books* a priest-confessor could find an appropriate penance for a specific sin. Thus, for example, if a person confessed the sin of theft, the confessor could consult his book to find the penitential remedy (usually several days, weeks, months or even years of fasting). The *Penitential Books* are, then, simply lists of sins together with a list of customary penances.

The system of private or tariff penance was quite different from the discipline of public canonical penance that had developed during the fourth through the sixth centuries. For one thing, it was entirely private in character; the penitent's confession of sins, the assigning of a penance, and the liturgical prayer for forgiveness (the "formula of absolution") were all done privately. Secondly, the ordinary minister of tariff penance was a priest, whereas the bishop usually presided over the process of reconciliation in public canonical penance. Thirdly, tariff penance could be repeated as often as one felt the need for it. The rule of a single penance during a person's lifetime did not apply. These three features—privacy, easier access to a priest-confessor, and repeatability—certainly helped to popularize tariff penance.

Where did this new form of tariff penance first appear? In recent decades this question has been studied by a number of liturgists and historians, and the most plausible theory is that tariff penance originated in the British Isles, more specifically in Ireland. Quite possible this "Irish penance" was brought onto the European continent by monk-missionaries. We know, for example, that a rather large number of monks came from Ireland to the European mainland under the leadership of St. Columban (ca. 543-615) during the late sixth and early seventh centuries. These men may very well have propagated a form of private penance that they had known and practiced in Ireland.

Once it had reached the continent, the system of Irish penance naturally underwent some modifications. Some of the penances contained in the *Penitential Books* seemed extravagantly severe, and a need arose to temper their harshness. In some places this need was satisfied through the system of "commutation," a method whereby the severity of penances was lessened or commuted. Several such methods of commutation arose—and not all of them were exemplary. One way to commute a tough penance, for example, involved making an offering to the local pastor for the purpose of having Masses celebrated for the sinner's forgiveness. In the hands of an unscrupulous priest, of course, this sort of commutation could have serious disadvantages for the penitent. There is a notorious example of a medieval pastor in the French town of Souest who discovered he could make the tariff system of penance profitable. He made most of his money in Lent when, according to medieval custom, husbands and wives were expected to abstain from sexual intercourse. If a penitent came to him and confessed he had departed from this discipline, the pastor would demand an offering for the purpose of having Masses celebrated. On the other hand, if a penitent came during Lent and vowed that he had kept the discipline of sexual abstinence, the pastor would accuse him of a sin of birth control—and demand money for Masses. Either way, the penitent lost!

Such abuses were obviously outrageous and local diocesan councils frequently condemned them. But other forms of commutation, some of them equally abusive, also existed. For instance, a penitent who felt he was unable to fulfill the assigned penance (because of ill health or extreme inconvenience) might hire a just man, usually a monk, to perform the penance in his stead. The penitent then made an offering to the monk's monastery in gratitude for services rendered. Still another method of commutation, this one far less reprehensible, involved changing a person's penance from *fasting* (the usual one) to *prayer* (often the seven penitential psalms or similar prayers).

All these methods of commutation reveal, once again, the search for forms of penance that are pastorally realistic. Poor people, for instance, would have been hard pressed to make an offering in order to substitute masses for weeks or months of fasting. The substitution of prayers in place of fasting was a more equitable solution and, as we shall see, this form of penitential activity became the ordinary procedure in private (tariff) penance. Still, the conveniences of the Irish system of penance—especially its privacy and its repeatability—made it popular throughout Europe. Moreover, while the public canonical system of penance was a process that involved several distinct stages (admission of sin and exclusion from the eucharist; a lengthy period of penance; and formal reconciliation with the community through prayer and the imposition of hands), private penance permitted the penitent to confess and be absolved in one simple rite.

Private penance also revealed a shift of emphasis in the theology of reconciliation. While public penance stressed the social nature of sin and reconciliation, private penance encouraged a more individualistic point of view. Furthermore, public penance had emphasized the notion that a Christian makes satisfaction for sin by doing works of charity and social justice (caring for the poor, visiting the sick and the imprisoned). But private penance tended to regard the very humiliation and embarrassment of making one's confession as the chief form of satisfaction for sin. In private penance, indeed, the actual works of penance were done only *after* the Christian had confessed and received absolution. The important sacramental gesture of reconciliation—the imposition of hands —gradually disappeared from private penance, even though technically it remained on the books until the sixteenth century and beyond.

Gradually, tariff penance—with its emphasis on private confession and absolution by the priest-confessor—replaced most other forms of reconciliation in Western Christianity. More and more frequently, confessors assigned prescribed prayers, rather than fasting or works of charity, as a Christian's penance to be performed after confession. In 1215, the ecumenical Fourth Lateran Council established a discipline that most Catholics today remember. The Council required all Catholics who had "reached the age of discretion" to confess their serious sins at least once a year to a priest and to receive holy communion at least during the Easter season. This annual confession mandated by the Fourth Lateran Council was, of course, that form of private penance we have just been discussing.

By the early thirteenth century, therefore, private penance had all but obliterated those forms of public penance known in earlier centuries of Christianity. Interestingly, however, the rituals for reconciling penitents on Holy Thursday often continued to appear in official liturgical books.

35

The term "confession"—originally used for *one part* of the reconciliation process—now began to designate the entire sacrament of penance. After the Reformation occurred in the sixteenth century, the Catholic church reacted vigorously against those reformers who denied that private penance was necessary, effective or important. In its decree on the sacrament of penance (November, 1551), the Council of Trent insisted that private confession was absolutely necessary for mortal sins, which had to be confessed to a qualified priest according to number, type, and special circumstances. Trent also insisted that the sacrament of penance was necessary for the salvation of persons who sinned seriously after baptism.

The requirements laid down by the Council of Trent are quite familiar to most Roman Catholics. Indeed, the decisions made at the Fourth Lateran Council and at Trent have been reiterated in official documents of the church down to the present day. Only at the Second Vatican Council were appreciable changes in the manner of celebrating Christian reconciliation mandated.

Vatican II's new Rite of Penance thus represents one stage of a long historical development. The three forms of celebration included in this new rite—individual, communal and communal with general absolution—manifest the influences of this long history.

For example, the rite for individual confession and absolution reflects the tradition of private penance that spread widely in Europe, especially after the start of the seventh century; the common services of penance (with opportunity for individual reconciliation or general absolution) recall some of the features associated with the public canonical penance practiced in the earlier centuries of Christian life. The new rite is thus a kind of mosaic fashioned out of the many historical ways Christians have sought and received the reconciliation offered by God at work in the life, death and resurrection of Jesus.

This last point is especially important in light of the historical outline offered in the present essay. If an attempt were made to summarize the history of penance in the church, the matter could be put this way: the history of penance is the history of Christians working to discover the *many* opportunities for reconciliation that are revealed in the life of faith. The history of penance is a history of *diversity* and *change,* of the continuing search for a pastoral strategy that is at once realistic and compassionate, challenging and practical. This history shows clearly that Christians have found reconciliation in many different ways. There is no single, magical way of doing penance which satisfies the needs of everyone, everywhere, at all times. The various forms for celebrating penance through the ages reveal the efforts Christians have made to lend flesh to Paul's words: "It was God who reconciled us to himself through Christ and gave us the work of handing on this reconciliation. In other words, God in Christ was reconciling the world to himself . . . and he has entrusted to us the news that we are reconciled" (2 Cor. 5:18-19).

References

Documents from Old Testament Times. Edited by D. Winton Thomas. New York: Harper Torchbooks, 1961.

CHAPTER THREE

Reconciliation Through the Prayer of the Community

Godfrey Diekmann, OSB

The wording of this essay topic, "reconciliation through prayer," is not meant to be sensational, though it may make some persons wonder or even become uneasy. We have been accustomed to thinking of being reconciled to God in the sacrament of penance specifically through the three acts of the penitent: sorrow for sin; confession and satisfaction (the "quasi-matter" of the sacrament, to use a well-known scholastic term); to which is added the priest's pronouncement of absolution, "I absolve you from your sins" (the "form" of the sacrament). That viewpoint, now well-entrenched, I would venture to call a *modern* viewpoint. It is only some 700 years old and, perhaps even more significantly, it is not now, and never has been, shared by the Eastern Church. They and we in the West for over a thousand years demand, of course, the sinner's conversion; that is, his will to change to God, his admission of guilt and his performance of penitential works. All this, however, means basically that the penitent is asking for and expressing his hope for forgiveness. The actual forgiveness itself is then granted by God; God is moved by prayer and particularly by the prayer of the people of God, by the *ecclesia mater*—the church or mother interceding for its erring members. Among those prayers of the people, the Our Father has pride of place. Another highly important fact has to be kept in mind in order to understand the reconciling and mediating role of the church—of the community of the people of God during much of the history of Christianity. Reconciliation was not considered solely as an occasional act tied, as it were, exclusively to the sacrament of penance. Reconciliation was understood, in its biblical sense, as equivalent ultimately to God's total work of redemption accomplished in Christ. As St. Paul says, God has reconciled us to himself by Christ Jesus (2 Cor. 5:18). People, though reconciled to God once and for all by the saving death of Christ, are nevertheless throughout their lives in continuing and daily need of that redemption becoming ever more operative in themselves. Men and women are in constant and enduring need of reconciliation. For, as Martin Luther insisted in one of his great spiritual insights, a person is always *simul justus et peccator,* both just and sinner. Reconciliation is a daily, ongoing, never ending process in the life of every man. Reconciliation is synonymous with Christian life, its constant and chief imperative. The fact that we, especially since the twelfth century in the West, have identified reconciliation so exclusively with the sacrament of penance as its single (if occasional) complete act has obscured our need of daily constant reconciliation as the very stuff and meaning of Christian existence on earth. And this in turn is, I believe, the most basic reason for our present dissatisfaction about our customary use and understanding of the sacrament of penance. The latter is unrealistic because it largely ignores the biblical message of constant daily reconciliation. Hence, my first purpose in this essay is to illustrate the biblical understanding of reconciliation which is reflected in what is likely the first non-biblical (i.e., non-canonical) Christian writing, the *Didache* or "Teaching of the Twelve Apostles." I think it may be safely regarded as among the most ancient of Christian writings.

In the *Didache* the message is clear: reconciliation is effected above all in the weekly Sunday celebration of the eucharist and by prayer, more particularly by the Our Father. Note that I have not said, "by the sacrament of penance." It is simply a fact of history that for at least six centuries, and likely much longer, the average devout Christian did not in the entire course of his life undergo the gradually developing and severe discipline of public or canonical penance. Of that public penance, which was always limited to a very few people and was granted only once in a lifetime, I shall speak later. I am now speaking of the normal process of reconciliation to God and neighbor as it was experienced by the vast majority of Christians in the six or more centuries closest to Christ. According to the *Didache,* reconciliation took place above all in the assembly of the Sunday eucharist. "Confess your sins that your sacrifice may be pure" (*Didache,* chapter 14). The *Didache*'s instruction naturally reminds us of Christ's command: "If you go and offer sacrifice, if you have something against your brother, go first and make peace with your brother" (Matthew 5:23). The *Didache* says "confess your sins." It goes without saying that this does not mean anything like our practice of private confession which was not known then and would not be known for many a long century. In all probability this confessing of sins meant mutual asking of forgiveness through the Lord's Prayer. The proof? The text of this prayer is given in chapter 8 of the *Didache.* And it includes the doxology "for thine is the kingdom," etc. Now this doxology was precisely a liturgical addition to the Our Father; it was an acclamation of the people added to public prayer. Other examples of such acclamations are to be found in chapters 9 and 10 of the *Didache,* where the eucharistic prayer is given. In other words, the Our Father had already become a public liturgical prayer. And since the Sunday eucharist was the only time the people gathered for worship, it would seem to follow necessarily that the Our Father with its petition of forgiveness was an integral part of the eucharistic service. This is certain, it seems to me, from what the author of the *Didache* says in chapter 4:14: "In the congregation (i.e., in the worshipping assembly) you shall confess your transgressions and you shall not betake yourself to prayer with an evil conscience."

Note that reconciliation with the brethren is therefore the basic presupposition as well as the function of both eucharist and prayer. Herein, of course, the author echoes the gospel of Matthew, where one finds Christ's command to be reconciled with one's brother before offering sacrifice (Matthew 6:14). A similar thing is found in the gospel of Mark: "And whenever you stand praying, forgive if you have anything against anyone, so that your Father also who is in heaven may forgive you your trespasses" (Mark 11:25). Prayer of its nature demands the will to reconcile; otherwise it is a mockery of God. If further proof of this point (viz., that the *Didache* means the Our Father when it speaks of confessing sins and finding forgiveness) is needed, I think it can be deduced from the *Didache*'s striking knowledge and preference for Matthew's gospel, especially the Sermon on the Mount, of which the Lord's Prayer is a part. It is the Matthean version of the Our Father that the *Didache* gives us verbatim in chapter 8. As is well known, Matthew sees the chief purpose and climax of the Lord's Prayer in the petition for mutual forgiveness. Immediately after giving the text of the Our Father, Matthew adds Christ's words "For if you forgive men their trespasses, your heavenly Father will also forgive you" (Matthew 6:14).

This earliest gospel interpretation of the Our Father as climaxing in the "forgive us as we forgive," together with this same interpretation in the public worship of the primitive church, throws significant light on the early Christian practice of reciting the Lord's Prayer daily. The author of the *Didache* enjoins such private praying of the Our Father three times each day. Surely the Our Father was also the great baptismal prayer, the renewal of the baptismal commitment to God as Father. But the early Christian was made keenly aware, at least three times every day, that God is "our Father," that reconciliation to one's neighbor was the only sign of reconciliation with the heavenly Father given by Christ. Thus the Lord's Prayer both in public and private recitation, became the Christian prayer, not simply one prayer among many others. It reminded believers that reconciliation with one's neighbor constitutes the very warmth and heart of Christian life.

St. Augustine echoes this same point of view: "The remission of sin takes place not solely in the sacred ablution of baptism, but in the daily recitation of the Lord's Prayer. In it you have, as it were, your daily baptism." For that reason, Augustine frequently admonishes his congregation to strike their breasts at the words "forgive us as we forgive" when the Our Father is said at mass. The Lord's Prayer therefore was the hallmark of a forgiving Christian. It was handed over with solemn ritual to the candidates for baptism, for they were to enter into a community of brothers and sisters. It had to be recited by them before they were permitted to be baptized. It was explained to them at length in the mystagogic catechesis immediately following the rites of initiation. It was demanded before the definitive prayer of reconciliation was recited in the name of all by the priest or bishop in public penance. It was required of him who was to be anointed. Every sacrament was a sacrament of reconciliation, of which the Our Father was the perfect verbal expression derived from our Lord himself. As Tertullian said, the Lord's Prayer is the *breviarium,* the epitomy of the whole gospel. And the gospel is a gospel of mutual love, of reconciliation.

Likewise, every hour of public prayer, of what is now called the Divine Office, climaxed with a final Our Father. St. Benedict brings this point home forcefully in his Rule by stating that at morning and evening prayer (Lauds and Vespers), the abbot of the monastery is to recite the Our Father aloud, so that all the monks may be aware of the phrase "forgive us as we forgive." In this way, there will be perfect reconciliation among the brethren at least every morning and evening.

But it was particularly in the eucharist, the source and center of all reconciliation, that the Lord's Prayer then, now and always, has occupied a climactic place and role. Its place sometimes varied. Sometimes it was said before the breaking of the bread, sometimes after; but it was always the introduction to the communion. We can still remember that from the old ritual for Good Friday. On that day the only preparation for communion was the praying of the Our Father. In fact, some authors have claimed that St. Gregory the Great believed that Christ consecrated the bread and wine by means of the Our Father. For is not the Our Father the prayer of the new covenant? True, the position of the Lord's Prayer before communion was also influenced by the petition "give us this day our daily bread," and by that was meant the eucharistic bread. But an equally urgent reason is the petition "forgive us as we forgive." St.

Augustine says that we pray the Our Father before communion so that "after these words 'forgive us as we forgive' we may approach the altar confidently (literally, 'with washed face')." The custom of washing before a meal was, then as now, a general practice. The Our Father, in Augustine's view, admitted Christians to the eucharistic meal because through this prayer they had "washed their faces."

Obviously these two petitions ("forgive us as we forgive" and "give us this day our daily bread") were not meant to be mutually exclusive. On the contrary, mindful of Christ's injunction not to approach the altar without forgiving our neighbor, we first forgive, in the Our Father, and therefore trustingly ask to be admitted to the table of holy bread. The Lord's Prayer is truly an "epitomy of the gospel." In it are contained a daily renewal of baptismal commitment, the desire for eucharist, and a daily and constant pledge of reconciliation. The spiritual climate established by the Our Father could, if good use were made of it, really effect the sort of community reconciliation which the church has always intended by it.

But there is another dimension to prayer as reconciliation. The word "reconciliation" still sounds somewhat negative: it conveys the sense of "clearing away hindrances or obstacles." But Christian reconciliation aims at something much more positive than that. It intends love, a reconciliation like that of the prodigal son, which included an embrace and a joyful banquet of renewed fellowship. Christian reconciliation, a loving reconciliation in Christ, necessarily demands a genuine concern for others. It demands a constantly alive and ever more sensitive awareness of responsibility toward them. A Christian social conscience in its deepest and widest dimensions—that is what reconciliation requires.

It is noteworthy that our earliest Christian documents outside the New Testament show exactly this kind of social concern in prayer. One such document, the "First Letter of Clement," written in the first century A.D., sheds light on this point. In chapters 59 and 60 of this "letter," we find an example of public prayer (possibly connected with the eucharist). The petitions found in this solemn public prayer mention "rescuing those in distress," "raising up the fallen," "assisting the needy," "healing the sick," "feeding the hungry," "releasing the captives," "reviving the weak," "encouraging those who lose heart," etc. This is a very comprehensive, very catholic list of petitions. In fact, it sounds very similar to the petitions contained, both now and in the past, in the Good Friday service. It is my conviction that petitions like these, similar to our "prayers of the faithful," provide an excellent opportunity for bringing about reconciliation in the positive sense of evoking a concern for the needs of others.

For example, would the Holocaust of the Jewish people in this century have occurred if we had *regularly* remembered their needs in prayer—as we do once a year in the solemn prayers of Good Friday?

This positive aspect of prayerful reconciliation is clearly demonstrated by the earliest and most traditional bodily gesture of prayer. There are authors who claim that bodily gestures are the most primitive features of any ritual. This is, I believe, correct. Certainly it is true as far as permanent teaching effectiveness is concerned. A gesture is far more effective than mere words. In any event, the early Christians followed the example of the Jews who prayed standing, with arms upraised to God. This custom of standing was expressly sanctioned by Jesus. It was also common throughout the entire Mediterranean basin; pagans likewise prayed to God in this manner. The Christians adopted a familiar practice but added something to it. Consciously and deliberately keeping their hands upraised, they extended their arms and explained that this was a sign of the cross of Christ who gave his life for all. In prayer, Christians put on the mind of Christ on the cross; they embraced everybody in the act of praying just as Christ embraced all human persons by extending his arms on the cross. For this reason Tertullian reminded Christians that by extending their arms in prayer they imaged Christ on the cross. And in the Odes of Solomon, a collection of early Christian hymns, the poet says: "I have stretched out my hands, for stretched-out arms are an image of the Savior." St. Ambrose echoes this tradition when he says that "you (Christians) should visibly demonstrate an image of Christ on the cross."

This theme and this stance of prayer prevailed in Christendom well into the Middle Ages. St. Thomas Aquinas summed it up in the following words: "The gestures of the hands are not just useless or silly customs; they are meant to signify Christ's extension of his arms on the cross." According to Aquinas, the priest extends his arms at mass in order to signify that his prayer is directed to God in supplication for the people. And this understanding of prayer was maintained in the rubrics which commanded that whenever the priest prayed in the name of the people, as in the collect, the preface and the eucharistic prayer, he should pray with arms extended. Rubrics, after all, have a way of tenaciously hanging on even though their meaning may have been lost or even distorted.

Public Penance

So far I have been dealing not with public penance but with the normal ways of being reconciled in the first centuries of the Christian Church. Père Gy, the noted French Dominican liturgist, summarizes the first six centuries of Christian reconciliation by saying that the daily faults and sins were understood to be forgiven by the normal ascetical and devotional practices of Christian life and prayer, especially the Our Father. We have already spoken of that. Gy also notes that the discipline which came to be called "public" or "canonical" penance was invoked only for major sins and crimes, especially those of a public or notorious nature. This discipline of public or canonical penance quite soon developed into three stages: the entrance into the penitential state; the time of public penance, which came to be associated especially with Lent after that season had taken form; and the actual rite of reconciliation itself. Reconciliation came especially to be associated with Maundy Thursday. In all three stages of public penance the prayer of the congregation played a decisive and essential role.

First, *the relation between community prayer and entrance into the penitential state.* Entrance into penance was not freely given; the genuineness of the will to conversion on the part of the penitent had to be clearly ascertained. So we are told, for example, that the sinner would stand at the entrance of the church and plead with the faithful to intercede for him that he might be officially enrolled in the order of penitents. As a matter of fact, Ambrose, Augustine and Jerome declared that participation by the faithful, that is, their common intercessory prayer, was so highly esteemed that to achieve it was a decisive reason why the sinner was willing to submit himself to this terribly severe discipline of public penance.

Second, *the relation between community prayer and the period of public penance itself.* A description of this time of penitential practice at Rome was supplied for us by the Greek church historian Sozomen in the later fifth century. He told how the penitents threw themselves on the floor of the church, how the bishop went with them, and how the whole congregation wept with them. After prayer, the bishop raised up the penitents, said a prayer over them in the name of the whole assembly and then dismissed them. This dismissal was accompanied by a laying on of hands. This dismissal of the penitents left traces in the Roman liturgy. The Lenten "prayer over the people," introduced with the words "bow your heads," took the place of what was earlier called explicitly *oratio super penitentes*, the "prayer over the penitents." In any event it was a prayer of all the church assembled for the penitents. Even more important, perhaps, was the intercession for penitents which always took place in the "prayers of the faithful." Tertullian tells us how vividly the congregation experienced this prayer for the penitents and how they embraced their erring brothers, for "Are we not all one body?" Augustine, especially, never ceased to encourage his congregation to intercede for those who by their public penance admitted their need of the mediating prayer of their spiritual family. And Ambrose made it clear that while the personal acts of the penitent (sorrow, tears) were essential, they are not adequate. Sorrow and tears must be accompanied by the tearful petitions of *mater ecclesia,* the Christian community.

Third, *the relation between community prayer and the act of reconciliation.* At the present, definitive reconciliation in the sacrament of penance is accomplished by the declarative sentence "I absolve you from your sins." This juridical statement by the priest became universal and obligatory in the West only after the Council of Trent. It had come into more or less general usage only in the twelfth century. Previously, that is for nearly two-thirds of the church's history in the West, reconciliation was effected by prayer plus the laying on of hands by the bishop or priest. Moreover, the prayer asking God's forgiveness, even though officially spoken by the bishop or priest, was understood to be the prayer of the entire Christian community. Their intercessions, their pleading for their brothers and sisters and their weeping were essential. God heard the sinner's plea and forgave his sins because of the prayers of the just. The evidence is overwhelming. Moreover, it is this crucial relationship between community intercession and reconciliation that has inspired our recent efforts to underscore the truly communal character of the sacrament of penance.

Evidence for the Community's Role in Reconciling

The East. The role of the entire community in reconciling penitents is attested by two important documents from the East: the *Didascalia* (third century) and the *Apostolic Constitutions* (fourth century). The *Didascalia* instructs that the bishop is to be told if someone sins and does penance; then, while the whole congregation prays for the sinner, the bishop imposes hands on him and the penitent is received back into fellowship with the church. The *Apostolic Constitutions* gives similar directions: after the sinner has demonstrated his sorrow, the bishop lays hands on him while all present pray. Once this is done, the penitent is allowed once more to enter the church.

The West: The evidence for the community's role in reconciling penitents is vast; here I will mention only the testimony of the greatest church Fathers. Writing in the third century, Tertullian tells penitents that the prayer of the church is the prayer of Christ himself. "When you prostrate yourself at the feet of the brethren," Tertullian noted, "It is to Christ that you extend your beseeching arms. To him you address your pleas; and when the brethren weep over you, Christ groans for you. Christ beseeches the Father for you." In fact Tertullian goes so far as to say "By the prayers of the people the penitent is loosed from his sins."

Similar evidence is found in the writings of Pope Cornelius (†253). In a letter to Fabian, bishop of Antioch, Cornelius said that when a certain public sinner had confessed his crime with groaning and tears, the entire community interceded for him and received him back into communion.

Ambrose continues the testimony in the fourth century. Whenever the entire church prays and weeps, it does so with the penitent. "The church," Ambrose observed, "has both water and tears for the forgiveness of sins: the water of baptism and the tears of penance." Ambrose was fond of the notion that the church is mother, one that weeps for her children. He therefore encouraged penitents to seek the help of the assembled holy people and to ask them to pray for him, "so that through them mother church will weep for you and wash away your sins with her tears." The tears of the church are like a second baptism for the penitent. "For Christ," Ambrose said, "desires that the many pray for the one." Commenting on the gospel story of the dead boy, the only son of the widow, Ambrose declares further: "If your sin is grave and you are incapable yourself of cleansing it by your tears of sorrow, then ask that your mother the church weep for you. The church intercedes for each one as if he were her only son." By "church" Ambrose did not mean some abstraction; he meant the living and participating Christian community: "Christ is most pleased when the many intercede for the one. The penitent is cleansed by the good works of all the faithful, and is washed from sin by the tears of the people. He is redeemed from sin by the prayers and sighs of the congregation. For Christ granted his church the gift to reconcile one person through all."

It should be noted that in these patristic texts we are dealing with the discipline of public penance, not with forgiveness of the daily minor faults. For these last there was also intercessory prayer, particularly (as we have seen) the Lord's Prayer.

But what of the *graviora*, the more serious and scandalous sins? On this point it may be useful to look at the testimony of St. Augustine. Augustine seems to have attributed reconciliation not only to the ministers of the church (bishop or priest) but to the *sancti*, the holy people of God as well. Both minister and people contribute to the process of reconciliation. While he often stresses the role of the priest, Augustine never ignores the indispensable role of community intercession for penitents. The praying people constitute the *ecclesia mater*, the mother church interceding for her children. Thus, for Augustine, the intercessory

46

power of the community of saints, of the congregation, is central. It is quite possible that Augustine's position was rooted in passages of Scripture like 1 John 5:16 and James 5:16; in both these texts, Christians are advised to confess their sins to one another and to pray for sinners.

Augustine's stress on the community's power of intercession gave theological expression to a practice that had long been current among Christians: the practice of appealing to "confessors" (persons who had suffered for the faith but had not been slain). The intercessory power of these community "heroes" was widely respected.

In any case Augustine's own respect for the prayer of the community in the process of reconciliation is undeniable. "God dwells in his holy temple, that is, his church," Augustine insisted; "Through them (believers), he forgives sins because they are his living temple." In commenting on Peter and on the "power of the keys," Augustine states that it is not only Peter but the whole church which, with him, binds and looses sin. To make his point even more forceful, Augustine remarks: "You bind; you also loose: for he who is bound is separated from your company; and in so far as he is separated, he is bound by you. When he is reconciled, however, he is loosed by you, for you pray to God for him."

Augustine's strong conviction about the community's power to bind and loose seems to have been shared by his contemporary, Jerome. Jerome says that the priest cannot restore any one member of the community to spiritual health unless or until all the members together weep with him. And Jerome adds a striking reason for this: a father (that is, the priest) may forget his son; but a mother (that is, the church, the community) pleads for her child with all her strength.

St. Leo the Great's testimony, in the fifth century, may be added to that of Augustine and Jerome. Leo remarks that the most complete pardon is obtained when the whole church as one prays for the penitent. By "church" Leo too means, concretely, the assembled community, priest and people. But already by Leo's time a shift of emphasis is noticeable, one that reflects the ever greater clericalization of the church. Instead of the prayer of the whole assembly, priest and people, the intercessory petition of the minister, the priest, began to receive more attention. And so, by the time of Gregory the Great in the early seventh century, the entire discipline of public penance is being described in terms of the intercession of the priest: the priest cleanses the sinner of fault by praying.

Still, as I have already mentioned, rubrics have a way of being tenacious. Truths, even if no longer understood, continue to find ritual expression. Thus, the notion that the entire church mediates forgiveness by prayer continued to find ritual expression in the act of solemn reconciliation on Maundy Thursday or (as in Spain) on Good Friday. According to a number of pontificals, on Maundy Thursday the penitents would form a living chain, hand to hand outside the church. The bishop would then take the first by the hand and lead them all into the church, into the community, while the people prayed the penitential psalms. In Spain, during the eighth and ninth centuries, the people's part was ritualized even more dramatically. On Good Friday a deacon would pray to God for forgiveness of the penitent. The people responded by crying out *Indulgentiam* (Lord, grant pardon) three times. This ritual was repeated three times, and each time the people cried out fervently *Indulgentiam!* At the very least, this rite shows how strongly the people felt about their role in the reconciliation process.

Another "remnant" of the people's role in reconciliation may be seen in what we now call the "formula of absolution." For many years these "formulas" were simply collects, prayers of petition to God to forgive sinners. But these collects were prayers of the whole church; they constantly mention *famuli tui* (your servants), *populi tui* (your people), *servi tui* (your servants). *All* are praying through the mouth of the priest; *all* are confident that their prayer will be heard and that the repentant sinner will be forgiven. Then, in the early Middle Ages, the collect form began to be replaced by a "deprecatory" or "optative" form: "May almighty God have mercy on you and forgive you your sins", or, "May the passion of our Lord, through the intercession of the Blessed Virgin and of all the saints. . . . " These deprecatory prayers still suggested the participation of all the people in the process of forgiveness. But by the twelfth and thirteenth centuries, even the deprecatory formulas began to be replaced by a declarative judgment made by the priest: "I absolve you." As has been seen, Trent made this "declarative judgment formula" obligatory: "I (the priest) absolve you (the penitent)."

When, a few years ago, the reform of the sacrament of penance was being discussed in Rome, a strong body of opinion favored a return to the earlier "deprecatory" formulas—for these formulas are universally used in the East. Unfortunately those who favored such a return did not prevail. The formula of absolution in the new Rite of Penance thus represents a compromise: it sets the declarative judgment ("I absolve you") in the context of a deprecatory formula which explicitly speaks of the forgiveness of sins "through the ministry of the church." And the old and venerable deprecatory prayer, "May the passion of our Lord Jesus Christ, the intercession of Mary and all the saints," is included at least as an alternative after the absolution.

48

Conclusion

The history and theology examined in this essay reveal quite strongly the role of community intercession in the process of reconciling penitents. Some may still want to ask: what words are absolutely essential for the validity of the sacrament of penance? I urge that this question never again be asked. That question has done more harm to sacramental theology through the centuries than almost any other. My plea throughout this essay has been for a recognition of the *fullness* of sacramental signs. Theologians commonly agree today that the first and immediate result of penance is full spiritual restoration, reconciliation with the church. I agree, but I would add that reconciliation with other people without their being aware of it or consenting to it does not make much sense. Perhaps that is why, in recent years, there has developed such an instinctive allergy against the customary rite of penance ("confession"). For, among people who took it seriously, confession may have dusted the angel's wings, but it seemed to do little to awaken the *social* conscience, the sense of responsibility toward the underprivileged. We were encouraged to strain at the gnat and we kept on swallowing the camel.

For quite a few centuries now, our rite of penance has been so private that it was most difficult to discern in it any evidence of its social or ecclesial dimension. In an address to pilgrims in Rome a few years ago, Pope Paul VI spoke of Christians "concelebrating" the eucharist, in some sense, with the priest. Church Fathers like Ambrose, Augustine and Jerome might have spoken of the people "concelebrating" the sacrament of reconciliation. For these men recognized that the people also "absolve," they also "bind and loose." The traditional image of the church as a matron with outstretched arms is realized in action in the sacrament of reconciliation, when the whole Christian assembly prays for its sinful members, trusting in God's promise of mercy and thus praying in an "infallible" way.

This, I submit, is the ancient and beautiful meaning of that problematic term *ex opere operato* (The sacrament effects grace by its very performance). Long before the term was invented, the church was actively engaged in its truest meaning: the entire community of believers pray for the sinner's forgiveness, and that prayer is heard infallibly by God since the church is nothing less than the body of Christ at prayer. Any renewal of pastoral practice in the sacrament of reconciliation must take this matter of community intercession into account. For we must never forget the New Testament injunction: "Pray for one another that you may be saved." Pray that you may be reconciled to God by being reconciled to one another.

CHAPTER FOUR

The Minister of Reconciliation: Some Historical Models

Raymond Studzinski, OSB

Ministers of reconciliation know from experience that people or events that have been negative influences on them may also have been influences for good in many unnoticed areas of their lives. Seldom are people or events simply good or evil in their effects upon us and so we all learn to live with and to appreciate the grey areas of our own personal histories. In this way, we come to more properly evaluate life in its varied shades.

This same process has application in the history of the sacrament of penance. We can see, for example, the negative witness in this area which came from monasticism and resulted in a view of the sacrament as a private affair. We may even wonder whether this negative influence is not all that we have left after the history of intertwining between monasticism and penance.[1] Likewise, even if we grant the negative effects of the Counter Reformation on the sacrament of penance—the minister of the sacrament perceived as a judge and the reduction of moral theology to casuistry— we may still wonder if that is the full picture of what happened to it during that period.[2]

Such pondering should encourage us to delve into the grey areas of the history of penance in search of positive insights and real gains in the practice and theology of the sacrament. What emerges as we engage in such research are models and guidelines for the minister of reconciliation which have gone relatively unnoticed and which are valuable today and should be understood. It is the purpose of this essay to gather some of these models and guidelines together and to offer them as a way of gaining perspective on the proper role and function of the minister of reconciliation.

I

Ours is an age in which technique has assumed great importance. Witness the large number of "how-to-do-it" books. They guarantee success at any number of roles and occupations. Of interest to our age would be one of the earlier "how-to-do-it" books for Christian conversion: the collection of sayings of the Desert Fathers known as the *Apophthegmata Patrum* (c. A.D. 300-600 in Syria, Palestine and Egypt).[3] These sayings of the Desert Fathers are interesting for the insight they give into the struggles of the early monks with the demonic, but for our purposes they are more interesting in the relationship which they describe as existing between the spiritual father and his disciple. It is this notion of spiritual paternity as it developed in the desert which should be helpful to the minister of reconciliation.

The recent instruction on the new Rite of Penance speaks in these words about the minister of reconciliation: "By receiving the repentant sinner and leading him to the light of the truth the confessor fulfills a paternal function: he reveals the heart of the Father and shows the image of Christ the Good Shepherd."[4] For a clearer understanding of this paternal function we can turn to the ancient tradition of desert monasticism. It was to the desert that the monk went to do battle with demonic forces of evil and sin. He was helped and guided in this struggle by an elder, one who had been through a like experience and thus had won for himself the title of *Abba* or Father. The dialogue between the *Abba* and his spiritual son consisted of a confession of doubt or an evil tendency on the part of the disciple and a response of wise counsel on the part of the spiritual father. An example: "A brother came to Abbot Pastor and said: 'Many distracting thoughts come into my mind and I am in danger because of them.' Then the elder thrust him out into the open air and said, 'Open up the garments about your chest and catch the wind in them.' But he replied, 'This I cannot do.' So the elder said to him, 'If you cannot catch the wind, neither can you prevent distracting thoughts from coming into your head. Your job is to say no to them.'"[5]

Another example offers the healing, reassuring nature of the dialogue: "An elder was asked by a certain soldier if God would forgive a sinner. And the elder said to him, 'Tell me, beloved, if your cloak is torn will you throw it away?' The soldier replied, 'No, I will mend it and put it back on.' The elder said to him, 'If you take care of your cloak, will God not be merciful to His own image?'"[6]

Modern man, as the disciple in the desert of old, is also looking for the life-giving word which will remove his doubt and thus help him to overcome evil. He comes to the minister of reconciliation with the hope of receiving it.

A basic belief in the desert was that man must break out of himself by a disclosure of his problem to an elder; this was the first step in the process of healing. Perhaps the most striking characteristic of the Desert

Fathers was their unique ability to elicit a confession from their disciples. This was not a matter of prying but rather a way of creating a situation and a relationship of trust wherein the disciple could open himself. If the disciple could articulate his problem, he could gain peace. 7 The spiritual father tried in every possible way to break down the walls of silent resistance. A well-known story illustrates this: "Makarios, the most celebrated authority of the Scetic desert, visits the young hermit Theopemptos, whom he knows to be in danger. Joyfully received, the father of monks asks, 'How is it with you?' Afraid to bare himself, the oppressed man replies with a formula of monastic courtesy: 'Due to your prayer it is well.' The old man then asks with greater urgency, 'Are you not being tempted in thought?' But the other insists, 'Up to now I have been well.' Here the old ascetic sheds his dignity. 'See, for many long years I have been practicing self-denial and all men honour me. Yet, though I am old, the daemon of lasciviousness still plagues me.' Now the younger man takes courage, 'Believe me, father, it plagues me, too!' In the same manner, Makarios declares himself exposed to other temptations until he moves the younger one to confession."8

In the above story, the spiritual father does not see himself apart from the struggle that is the lot of all men converting to God. He is in touch with himself and his own struggles; he can even be somewhat transparent about them. The minister of reconciliation can, by his own deep awareness of his sinful condition, approach his penitents with a similar receptivity and perceptive presence.

The sayings of the Desert Fathers are noted for their compassionate character. This compassion springs from the Desert Fathers' deep self-awareness and appreciation of the human limitations of life. They were aware that confession and penitential deeds were only the human part of the divine healing process—it is God, after all, who converts and forgives sinners. Taking their clue from the gospel account of Jesus and the woman caught in adultery, they overcame sinful isolation and brought about reconciliation not by human judgment but by deeds and words of love. The following story is illustrative of this compassion which comes of self-knowledge: "A brother in Scete happened to commit a fault, and the elders assembled and sent for Abbot Moses to join them. He, however, did not want to come. The priest sent him a message, saying, 'Come, the community of brethren is waiting for you.' So he arose and started off. And taking with him a very old basket full of holes, he filled it with sand and carried it behind him. The elders came out to meet him and said, 'What is this, Father?' The elder replied, 'My sins are running out behind me, and I do not see them, and today I come to judge the sins of another!' They, hearing this, said nothing to the brother but pardoned him."9

The refusal to enter into judgment is also indicated in this short saying: "An elder said, 'Do not judge a fornicator if you are chaste, for if you do, you too are violating the law as much as he is. For He who said you shall not fornicate also said you shall not judge.'" 10

In a similar vein are the action and words of the Desert Father in the following account: "One of the brethren had sinned, and the priest told him to leave the community. So then Abbot Bessarion got up and walked out with him, saying, 'I too am a sinner!'" 11

The Desert Father's words were intended to be liberating. They were words designed to give hope of the attainment of salvation and to give guidance in the disciple's ongoing conversion. Often they were a supportive promise of prayerful intercession and activity on behalf of the disciple. The spiritual father by his life-giving words both hoped to ease a distressed conscience and to bring about a purifying movement leading to deepened insight.12 Consider this event: "A brother asked an old man, saying, 'What shall I do, father, for I do nothing a monk should, but in a kind of heedlessness I am eating and drinking and sleeping and always full of bad thoughts and great perturbation, going from one task to another and from one thought to another?' And the old man said, 'Sit in your cell and do what you can, and be not troubled; for the little that you do now is even as when Antony did great things and many in the desert. For I have this trust in God that whoever sits in his cell for His name and keeps his conscience shall himself be found in Antony's place.13'"

The concern of the Desert Fathers throughout their confessional method was that their disciples might patiently come to discover the truth of themselves. 14 Patience and truth were two important watchwords. The man who seeks the truth becomes independent of human approval and esteem. Dangers beset man in this pursuit of the truth. False humility, a focus on faults which do not really exist, would be to the detriment of legitimate and needed concern for real faults. Truth is ascertained in the real world; the desert tradition saw to it that man stayed in touch with reality. This appreciation of reality is evidenced in the warning against the human tendency to prematurely end the pursuit of truth. The penitent is cautioned to wait patiently through affliction and struggle until he has gained a deep and penetrating experience of what life with God means. Underlying this recommendation is the perception that life is never without its pain and difficulty. The struggle with evil is a lifelong pursuit which requires the complete self-engagement of the individual. Overconcern with hidden and unknown sins can be another escape from reality. Granted that sin extends beyond man's consciousness of it, it does not however extend beyond the reach of grace from which nothing is hidden. Grace is operative in life's experiences and produces healing at man's inmost depths. The focus of the penitent should not be inward but outward to life and to the events and experiences which life brings. Confession in the desert tradition does not foster introspection but supports a healthy and spontaneous involvement with others and with one's own destiny.15

The whole of the desert experience—a relentless quest for the truth exercised with extraordinary patience—sought to make humans conscious of all that was false and sinful in themselves. Truth stood before conscience, driving man to admit his sinful deeds. Truth penetrates and unfolds the relationship between man's deeds and his essential being. The requirement that truth lays down is that man maintain a congruence between his deeds and his essential being as from God and returning to God. This is nothing other than a call for man to be truthful to himself. Man is to see his essential being as that of real beauty because it has been shaped by the hand of God; this inner core of man is the seat of tranquility, of hope and belief, of true freedom. In truth man sees his own inner darkness as that which in actuality is far removed from his essential being.

Confrontation with the truth starts a conversion process. Conversion brings about a full admission of guilt and a willingness to be wholly at the service of the truth. Man finds himself then in a movement toward liberation and a future filled with possibilities. The greatest of these possibilities is salvation itself with its promise of complete fulfillment. The movement toward salvation has begun in time with the sight of the truth but finds its full culmination in eternity. Brought face to face with the truth in the now of temporal existence, man experiences his own confessional judgment. As he does so, he also experiences grace and so anticipates his final judgment and his hoped for glory. The confession which man is driven to in his encounter with the truth brings liberation and eternal life.

Here on earth the spiritual father hoped that his disciple would achieve tranquility. This was a state of final integration attained when the disciple possessed purity of heart—the ability to always see himself as made for the Other and to order everything in his life to that Other. The tranquil disciple sees the will of God for him as whatever facilitates his relationship with God. All activity is now prompted by the Spirit and this deepens the tranquility and peace which the disciple experiences. The disciple comes to rest in the God who is his tranquility.

Thus, the disciple has found the meaning of life in tranquility. He now embraces his vocation to holiness in that particular state in life truly and properly his. He has arrived at this point through the often painful process of discernment which he learned at the feet of his spiritual father. His confessions were for the purpose of learning to distinguish the pulls of evil in himself from the genuine movements of God's grace. No longer were his own pride, vanity or obsessive illusions entangled in what was his perception of God's will. In his relationship with the spiritual father the disciple had confronted and removed any false assertiveness, any defensiveness, and any false passivity. The disciple who had persevered acquired the confidence and the freedom that comes to the humble man who places his trust in God.

The spiritual father stood before his disciple as one who had already confronted the truth of himself and come to rest in God. The spiritual father open to the Spirit was a man guided by love rather than by external or logical norms. He acted with wisdom and insight. He had learned to lead by example rather than by laws or external prescriptions: "A brother said to Abba Poemen: 'Some brothers are living with me: do you wish me to command them?' The old man replied, 'Not at all. Act first, and if they wish to 'live,' they will put the lesson into effect themselves.' The brother said, 'Abba, they themselves want me to command them.' The old man said, 'No, become a model for them, and not a lawgiver.'"[16]

The spiritual father did not rest content with stock answers; he had reached the stage of learned ignorance. Consequently he approached the scriptures and all of life with freshness and vitality. The following story highlights this trait as that which distinguishes the spiritual father from the disciple: "Some elders once came to Abbot Anthony, and there was with them also Abbot Joseph. Wishing to test them, Abbot Anthony brought the conversation around to the Holy Scriptures. And he began from the youngest to ask them the meaning of this or that text. Each one replied as best he could, but Abbot Anthony said to them, 'You have not got it yet.' After them all he asked Abbot Joseph, 'What about you? What do you say this text means?' Abbot Joseph replied, 'I know not!' Then Abbot Anthony said, 'Truly Abbot Joseph alone had found the way, for he replies that he knows not.'"[17]

Above all, the spiritual father was one who had learned to love. He possessed a love which, because it regarded the other as another self, had enough humility and reverence to approach the interior life of the other without violating it or treating the other as an object. Such a love, of course, had demanded a complete inner transformation in the spiritual father, accomplished through a long process of renunciation: "After renunciation of the love of money, it is necessarily required of him that he strip himself of the love of praise. Then after that it is possible for him to be in the virtue of understanding: in humility and patience, in quietitude and lucidity of spirit, in the joy of his hope, in the vigilance of noble concerns, in the perfect love of God and of men: by these things he will come to purity of soul which is the crowning of the conduct God has enjoined upon man to attain in this life." [18]

The minister of reconciliation may not have as venerated a position before the penitent as did the spiritual father before the disciple, but the minister too must "father" the truth in his penitent. The minister's effectiveness in doing this will be enhanced to the degree that he has weathered the storm of his own conversion and come into a tranquil awareness of his real self. Because he values the liberated life he now experiences, he will speak words which are liberating and life-giving. His remarks will lead the penitent toward the development of discernment. His humility before the mystery of God and the mystery of evil will keep him realistic and more sensitive to the movement of the Spirit. His love will engender love and so bring the other to full maturity.

II

The introduction to the new rite of penance mentions various pastoral abilities needed by the minister of reconciliation: "In order to fulfill his ministry properly and faithfully the confessor should understand the disorders of souls and apply the appropriate remedies to them. He should fulfill his office of judge wisely and should acquire the knowledge and prudence necessary for this task by serious study, guided by the teaching authority of the Church and especially by fervent prayer to God. Discernment of spirits is a deep knowledge of God's action in the hearts of men; it is a gift of the Spirit as well as the fruit of charity." [19]

We have already seen how some of these pastoral abilities were utilized in the desert. Those insights of the desert tradition were carried on and developed in the monastic tradition. In fact the abbot's relationship to the monk, as described in the *Rule of Benedict* (c. A.D. 500), offers another possible model for the interaction of confessor and penitent. What is described in the Rule does not pertain directly to the sacramental order; nevertheless, the setting is sacral and has other features which enable us to make application to the ministry of reconciliation.

The monk is enjoined in chapter seven of the Rule not to hide any of his evil thoughts and tendencies from his abbot. [20] This injunction implies that the abbot functions analogously as a confessor in receiving these intimate revelations of his monks. In the chapter of the Rule about those who have been excommunicated for some serious fault, we have a description of the pastoral attitude which the abbot should have. The abbot is encouraged to act as the wise physician using every remedy that he has available. Furthermore, he is reminded that he has charge over those who are weak. His is not a lordship over the strong. He is presented with the model of the Good Shepherd as one who had pity on weakness and gave all the support and help that he could.[21]

In the chapter on the election of the abbot he is advised to place mercy over judgment, to act with prudent moderation, to strive to be loved rather than feared. The abbot is cautioned not to allow himself to become too upset or anxious, overbearing or obstinate, jealous or too suspicious. Above all, the abbot is encouraged to practice discretion— "the mother of the virtues." [22] Here we find a point especially helpful for contemporary pastoral practice.

The word "discretion" has its etymological roots in a Greek word meaning to differentiate, to discern, or to decide. When discretion is enjoined in the Rule, it is to be understood as a discernment of what will best lead to an experience of God.[23] Benedict saw as a goal of the monastic life an awareness of the presence of the risen Lord. This awareness came in those holy moments of life when the monk received a consoling, experiential knowledge of God. To act with discretion was to act in a way that made possible such continuing experiences. The Prologue of the Rule speaks both of the experience and the process leading to it: "The Lord looks for His workman among the masses of men. He calls to him: 'Who is the man that will have life, and desires to see good days?' And if, hearing this, you answer, 'I am he,' God says to you, 'If you desire true and everlasting life keep your tongue from evil and make sure your lips speak without guile; renounce evil and do good; seek peace and pursue it. If you do this, My eyes will see you, and My ears will hear your prayers. And before you can call out to Me, I will say to you: Behold, I am here. What can be more pleasing, dear brothers, than the voice of the Lord's invitation? See how He shows us the way of life in His benevolence'" [24]

The principles articulated here, of course, extend beyond the monastic context. The discernment process in every Christian's life should be directed toward fostering an ever increased awareness and experience of God's presence. The end sought by every Christian is the full experience of the Lord which is called vision. Benedict's analysis of man's pursuit of this experience is instructive. In the passage cited from the Rule, Benedict describes the Lord's revelation of himself as a "calling out" in the events of life. The response to that call of the God who says "Behold, I am here," is a deeper involvement in conversion. A person is to discover what is congruent in his life with the experience of God's presence and to eliminate those things which are not congruent with it. In this way he invites further experiences of the Lord.

What is striking about this approach to Christian conversion is its positive orientation. It is grace-centered rather than sin-centered. Man is encouraged to notice what fits with grace and what does not in order to invite still further grace. Underlying this positive approach is the belief that God is calling every person to a fuller experience of himself or herself and that each has the capacity to make a corresponding response to that call. What is required in this approach is an intense form of listening and pondering of attitudes and experiences in the face of God's presence. The result is that life becomes directed, totally taken hold of and thrust in the direction which the experience of the presence of the Lord has indicated.

The minister of reconciliation, while he is necessarily concerned with the sins of his penitent, should not overlook his penitent's grace experience. In this way he can give his penitent a positive approach to Christian conversion. Likewise the celebration of reconciliation can be clearly seen as a celebration of grace and not as depression over sin. As the abbot in the monastic context is a sacrament of the fatherhood of God, so the minister of reconciliation should be a sacrament of that fatherhood by his compassionate and uplifting presence to his penitent.

III

The friendly nature of the relationship between penitent and confessor is suggested in the introduction to the new rite in its comments about welcoming the penitent: "The priest should welcome the penitent with fraternal charity and, if the occasion permits, address him with friendly words."[25] In the writings of Francis de Sales (1567-1622), we have a number of indications as to the importance of the friendly tone of the relationship in the ministry of penance. DeSales claims that friendship provides the best context for the growth and development of the penitent. He counsels confessors to strive to be a friend to the penitent and to let themselves be loved as persons and not regarded as simply possessors of sacramental power. The relationship which De Sales describes is reciprocal; so De Sales also advises the penitent to approach the confessor with the confidence that one would place in a friend.[26]

The tone of friendship influenced the method De Sales used in responding to his penitents. From his writings we know that his confessional responses were not of the nature of regulations or orders but simply friendly advice. Because he assumed that his penitents had a strong desire for moral goodness, he did not believe they would benefit from having something imposed on them by another. His great respect for the freedom of the individual led him to support that freedom in whatever way it was moved to God. Such support did not call for legislation or endless detail. De Sales once remarked to his friend and penitent Jane Frances de Chantel: "I have often told you that one should certainly not go too much into detail with the exercise of virtue; rather, one ought to proceed quickly, candidly, childishly, in good faith, *grosso modo.*"[27]

Basically De Sales' approach was indirect and allowed the penitent himself a major role in ascertaining what God was asking in his conversion. This approach bolstered the self-esteem and sense of dignity of the penitent. It recognized the individual's uniqueness and allowed her to follow the pattern of growth proper to self. De Sales paid attention to the penitent's feelings and made appeal to them as a way of strengthening the will in its quest for God. He would elicit positive feelings not only for such things as the sufferings of Christ but also toward himself as confessor and friend as a way of drawing the penitent toward God. This affective educational method was indicative of De Sales' genius. It contributed to his success in drawing the whole man from the morass of sin into the sphere of God's merciful love.

Like De Sales every minister of reconciliation must find his own unique way of best responding to his penitents. He must bear in mind that the sacrament of reconciliation is intended to be a warm human encounter in which God's healing grace is bestowed. What we have presented from the desert, the monastic and the Counter-Reformation traditions are simply models of similar interaction. Many others could be presented. The three presented here were chosen because they brought to the center of attention the specifics of confessional method, the value of a positive orientation and the nature of the confessor-penitent relationship. The history of penance is indebted to the Desert Fathers and to monasticism for valuable insights into spiritual paternity and the dynamics and goal of confession; it is indebted to the Counter-Reformation for a deeper appreciation of warmth and other human feelings in the sacramental encounter. Of course, the scriptures continue to stand as a primary source of insight, of models and guidelines. The Letter to the Philippians underlines the humility which must mark any exercise of Christian ministry. Paul himself stands as a model of the minister of reconciliation:

For His sake I have suffered the loss of all things and count them as refuse, in order that I may gain Christ. Not that I have already obtained this or am already perfect; but I press on to make it my own, because Christ Jesus has made me His own. Brethren, I do not consider that I have made it my own; but one thing I do, forgetting what lies behind the straining forward to what lies ahead, I press on toward the goal for the prize of the upward call of God in Christ Jesus. Let those of us who are mature be thus minded; and if in anything you are otherwise minded, God will reveal that also to you. Only let us hold true to what we have attained (Phil. 3:8, 12-16).

Notes

1. See the discussion of monastic influences on penance in John T. McNeill and Helen M. Gamer's *Medieval Handbooks of Penance.* New York: Columbia University Press, 1938, pp. 23ff.

2 See the fine essay by the late Robert E. McNally, S.J., "The Counter-Reformation Views of Sin and Penance," *Thought,* LII (1977), 151-166.

3 Three recent translations of the Sayings are available: *The Sayings of the Desert Fathers.* Trans. by Benedicta Ward. Kalamazoo, Michigan: Cistercian Publications, 1975; *The Wisdom of the Desert.* Trans. by Thomas Merton. New York: New Directions, 1960; and *The Desert Fathers.* Trans. by Helen Waddell. London: Collins, 1962.

4 *Rite of Penance.* Hales Corners, Wisconsin: Sacred Heart Monastery 1957, p. 14.

5 *The Wisdom of the Desert,* p. 43.

6 *Ibid.,* p. 76.

7 On this point and for the whole phenomenon of desert confession, see H. Dörries, "The Place of Confession in Ancient Monasticism" in *Studia Patristica,* Vol. V, Edited by F.L. Cross. Berlin: Akademie-Verlag, 1962, pp. 284-311.

8 Cited in Dörries, p. 288.

9 *The Wisdom of the Desert,* p. 40.

10 *Ibid.,* p. 41.

11 *Ibid.,* p. 40.

12 Thomas Merton has done a careful study of this process used by the desert fathers from the standpoint of spiritual direction. See his essay "The Spiritual Father in the Desert Tradition" in his work, *Contemplation in a World of Action.* Garden City, N.Y.: Image Books, 1973, pp. 282-305.

13 *The Desert Fathers,* pp. 103-105.

14 Cf. Dorries, pp. 299-307.

15 The basis for this section is a fifth century work by Simeon of Mesopotamia, commented on by Dorries, pp. 298-308.

16 Cited in Merton, "The Spiritual Father in the Desert Tradition," pp. 302-303.

17 *The Wisdom of the Desert,* p. 52.

18 Cited in Merton, "The Spiritual Father in the Desert Tradition," p. 293.

19 *Rite of Penance,* pp. 13-14.

20 *The Rule of St. Benedict.* Trans. by Anthony C. Meisel and M.L. del Mastro. Garden City, N.Y.: Image Books, 1975, pp. 59-60.

21 *Ibid.,* pp. 72-73.

22 *Ibid.,* p. 100.

23 Cf. on this point August M. Raabe, "Discernment of Spirits in the Prologue to the Rule of Benedict," *American Benedictine Review* XXIII (1972), pp. 397-423.

24 *The Rule of St. Benedict,* pp. 43-44.

25 *Rite of Penance,* p. 16.

26 Francis de Sales, *Introduction to the Devout Life.* Trans. by John K. Ryan. Garden City, N.Y.: Image Books, 1955, pp. 41-43.

27 Francois Vincent, *Saint Francois de Sales,* Paris, 1923, p. 415, cited in Erik Berggren, *The Psychology of Confession.* Leiden: Brill, 1975, p. 52.

CHAPTER FIVE

The Table of Eucharist: Christian Fellowship and Christian Forgiveness

Nathan Mitchell, OSB

The second essay in this volume drew attention to the intimate relation between Christian baptism and Christian penance. There it was noted
that a change in the church's baptismal policy—the shift from adults to
children as a pastoral norm—produced a change in the practice of penance as well. The present essay seeks to explore another sacramental relationship: the link between the *eucharist,* the bread and cup of reconciliation, and the *forgiveness of sins.* In the liturgical history of the Christian churches this relationship has been expressed in a remarkable variety
of ways. Some of those ways will be discussed in the pages that follow.

Jesus: The Invitation to Kingdom and Table
Scripture scholars today are in almost unanimous agreement about one
significant fact: the central message of Jesus' preaching was the kingdom
or reign of God. This message comes across most powerfully in his use
of parables. It must be remembered that parables, as Jesus used them,
were not simply pious stories or colorful illustrations aimed at illiterate,
simple-minded folks. A parable is more like a hand grenade than a folk-
tale: it explodes people's customary ways of thinking and acting, and
challenges them to make basic choices, decisions that will utterly change
their lives. There is a provocative, subversive side to Jesus' parables. In
these apparently harmless stories there is explosive potential: the irre-
sponsible younger son squanders his father's money but is received back
with music and feasting, while the older son, dutiful and hard-working,
gets nothing special at all (Luke 15:11-32). Or again, the Samaritan, who
belonged to a class of people Jesus' contemporaries regarded as loathsome,
turns out to be the good man, while prominent religious leaders are cal-
lous and uncaring (Luke 10:29-37). As Jesus used them, the parables
are dramatic calls to decision about the kingdom itself, for the kingdom
is open to anyone who will listen, even "disreputable" and "polluted"
people like lepers, tax collectors and prostitutes.

Jesus' ministry was not limited, however, to the preaching of parables.

Another prominent aspect of his work seems to have been that of table fellowship. Just as Jesus invited even disreputable sinners to share the blessings of the kingdom, so also he invited those sinners to sit with him at table. Both kingdom and table were symbols of the joyful forgiveness God was offering people in the person and ministry of Jesus. Thus Jesus' approach to table fellowship was as subversive as his use of parables. At table he welcomed the very persons his contemporaries reproached as unclean: "While he was at dinner in the house it happened that a number of tax collectors and sinners came to sit at the table with Jesus and his disciples. When the Pharisees saw this, they said to his disciples, 'Why does your master eat with tax collectors and sinners?' When he heard this he replied, 'It is not the healthy who need the doctor, but the sick. Go and learn the meaning of the words: What I want is mercy, not sacrifice. And indeed I did not come to call the virtuous, but sinners '" (Matthew 9:10-13).

In his ministry, then, Jesus combined two important items. He joined his proclamation of the kingdom with the intimacy of table fellowship — i.e., he combined parable in word (preaching) with parable in action (meal). Secondly, Jesus united the intimacy of table fellowship with the joyful news that sins are forgiven. By welcoming sinners at table Jesus was saying, in effect: your sins are forgiven; the kingdom of God is open to you.

As modern scripture scholars have noted, the ministry of the table did not cease at Jesus' death. Those who believed in his message and experienced his risen presence continued to gather, to eat and drink, to proclaim the joyful news of forgiveness. The table became a crucial link between the earthly ministry of Jesus and the earliest mission of the Christian church. Through the fellowship of the table, Christians continued to experience Jesus' invitation to faith and forgiveness. Table and kingdom became signs of a reconciled existence, of a final communion in life and love to which all men and women are destined. In the common sharing of bread and cup Christians experienced the power of God at work in Christ to reconcile the world.

The connection between table and reconciliation, eucharist and forgiveness of sins, found a variety of expressions in the worship of the Christian community. We turn now to some of those liturgical expressions.

Jewish Background

In the last several decades, historians of the liturgy have become increasingly aware of the influence Jewish worship has had on the formation of public prayer in the Christian church. Christian worship was not created out of nothing; it developed and grew out of the tradition familiar to Jesus' own people. For example, the early Christian eucharist, a joyful meal dominated by themes of praise and thanksgiving for God's mighty deeds, has an obvious ancestry in the common meals shared by Jews: the weekly sabbath meal on Friday evening, the annual Passover supper that commemorated Israel's liberation from slavery in Egypt, the formal meals shared occasionally among friends or between a teacher and his disciples. Similarly, the Christian custom of praying at specified times of day and night (morning and evening; the third, sixth and ninth hours) seems to be rooted in familiar Jewish patterns of daily prayer in the synagogue.

It should not be surprising, then, to discover that both the structure and content of the Christian eucharist were shaped by traditional Jewish understandings of prayer, meal and sacrifice. Louis Ligier, a professor at the Gregorian University in Rome, has made extensive studies of the relation between Jewish liturgical prayers and Christian ones. It may be useful to present some of Ligier's conclusions here, since they are widely accepted by liturgists today.

1. *The Jewish grace after meals and the eucharistic prayer of Christians.* Ligier's studies have convinced him that there is a very close connection between the traditional Jewish grace after meals (called the *birkat ha-mazon*—literally, "blessing of the bread") and the early Christian eucharistic prayers. The great Jewish themes of thanksgiving—for God's goodness revealed in the land, in food and in forgiveness—are also found in early Christian eucharistic texts. Here, slightly abbreviated, is a Jewish grace after meals prayed at the conclusion of the Passover supper:

> Blessed are you, Lord our God, King of the universe! You
> feed us and nourish the whole world with goodness and grace,
> kindness and mercy. Blessed are you, Lord, who nourish all!

> We give you thanks, Lord our God, because you gave us as an
> inheritance a land that is wide, good and fruitful, because
> you gave us the Law and the Covenant, life and food.

> And for all these things we give you thanks and we bless your
> name, now and forever. Blessed are you, Lord, for the land
> and for the food.

> Our God and God of our Fathers, remember the Messiah, the

son of David your servant! Remember Jerusalem, the city of
your holiness; remember all your people, the house of Israel.
Grant prosperity, grace, kindness and mercy, life and peace
on this festival day of unleavened bread. Remember us in our
day, Lord our God; visit us in blessing and save us for life.
By your word of salvation and mercy, spare us and forgive
us: because our eyes are turned to you, O God, a gracious
and merciful King.

Blessed are you, Lord our God, King of the universe: Our
Father, our King, our Creator, our Redeemer! Remember us
every day and increase your grace and kindness toward us.

Strong echoes of this beautiful Jewish meal prayer are heard in one of
the earliest Christian eucharistic texts, the one found in the *Didache*
(Teaching [of the Twelve Apostles]), a small manual of catechesis and
liturgical practice that dates from the late first or early second century.
There we find the following Christian grace after meals:

We give you thanks, holy Father, for your holy name, which
you have planted in our hearts! We thank you for the knowledge, the faith and the undying life which you have revealed
to us through Jesus, your servant. Glory to you forever!

Almighty Lord, you have created all things for your name's
sake, and you give food and drink to people so that they
might enjoy them and give you thanks. But to us you have
given the spiritual food and drink of everlasting life through
Jesus, your servant.

Above all else, we give you thanks because you are mighty.
Glory to you forever!

Remember your church, Lord: deliver it from evil, perfect it
in your love, and gather it together from the four winds into
the kingdom you have prepared. Yours are glory and power
forever! Amen!

Just as the Jewish prayer praised God for land, food, nourishment and
mercy, so the Christian prayer thanks God for food and drink, for love
and mercy and for the undying life revealed in Jesus. The pattern and

65

the themes of these two prayers are unmistakably related. The major difference is that Christians add the person of "Jesus, your servant" to the list of gifts for which God is praised. Both prayers ask God to *remember* his people. "Remember," in this context, is a very strong verb that means not simply "recall," but "continue to act on behalf of." In both the Jewish and the Christian prayer God is asked to *continue acting in the present* by giving people nourishment, life and mercy.

These examples support Louis Ligier's notion that the eucharistic prayers of the Christian community took shape under the influence of traditional Jewish forms of worship. At the common table, through the sharing of bread and cup, both Jews and Christians acknowledged the continuing action of God on their behalf.

2. *The influence of the Jewish notion of sacrifice for sin.* Father Ligier's studies have also led him to the conclusion that Jewish understandings of sacrifice for sin have contributed to the Christian idea that the eucharist, the community's sacrifice of praise and thanksgiving, forgives sin. At first the idea that the eucharist forgives sin may sound unorthodox. So a few words of explanation are in order here. Many of us grew up with the assumption that the eucharist is for "good people only," not for sinners. We were carefully instructed that the appropriate sacrament for sinners is *penance.* Many can remember being told that the eucharist forgives venial sins, but that a person who receives communion in the state of mortal sin commits an outrageous sacrilege. For this reason, Catholics were often reluctant to approach the eucharist unless they had first gone to confession and received absolution.

We have to remember that, in the early centuries of Christian life, believers did not always look at the sacraments in quite the same way as we do. In the not-so-distant past, for instance, sacraments were often viewed as a quantitative system of actions which produce things (grace, virtue) which were not there before. According to this point of view, for example, the sacrament of penance produces or restores the grace and divine life that had been lost by sin. Similarly, marriage produces something: a sacred contract that makes it legitimate for a man and a woman to live together and raise a family.

In an earlier age Christians did not view the sacraments as productions, but as public moments of praise and thanksgiving that celebrated God's memory of his people, his abiding action among them. Sacraments were thought of as *verbs* (continuing action), not as nouns (things, objects). The church regarded itself as a community of persons who *remember* and who *are remembered.* The sacraments were the church's memory, and that memory was something *fleshly*. When Christians remembered God in the sacraments they *ate* and *drank*, they *washed* new members and *smeared* them with oil, they *laid on hands* for healing and forgiveness. Sacraments were the Christian community's way of "thinking with its skin," of "remembering with its body." When the church remembered, it did not hold seminars on obscure theological topics; it performed physical deeds of eating, drinking, washing and anointing.

Human memory can sometimes be lost, at least in part, and the church's memory is no different. From time to time in history, a part of the Christian memory gets lost and the need to rediscover it arises. The eucharist provides a convenient illustration of this point. For several centuries Christians seemed to forget that the eucharist is an action which demands the vigorous, intelligent participation of *all* believers. The reforms of the Second Vatican Council represented an effort to reawaken the church's sacramental memory by creating forms of worship which invite people to participate actively and intelligently. How successful these reforms will be remains to be seen, but their intent is certainly praiseworthy. For a church that loses its sacramental memory also loses touch with its very reason for existing.

The connection between the eucharist and the forgiveness of sins is perhaps one of those "lost memories" that needs rediscovering. That is why the work of scholars like Louis Ligier is important for people who are anxious to explore just what it means for the church to "remember" by "making eucharist." As we shall see, there is a strong tradition of Christian faith that regards the eucharist as a powerfully effective symbol of reconciliation and forgiveness. To say this is not to deny the importance or the legitimacy of sacramental penance in Christian life. It is simply to point out that Christians past and present have sought reconciliation in a variety of ways. Sacramental penance is one of those ways; eucharist is another; prayer, fasting and works of charity are still another. Thus, the important thing to notice is that Christians have experienced forgiveness through a rich diversity of actions: through the preaching of the Word; through the church's ministry of penance; through prayer; through deeds of social justice; through the table-fellowship of eucharist. All these actions form part of the church's mission to proclaim the good news of reconciliation (see 2 Corinthians 5:18-21).

With these points in mind, let us return to Ligier's idea that Jewish traditions about prayer and sacrifice influenced the early Christian understanding of the relation between eucharist and forgiveness of sins. Ligier has based his position on the prayers that gradually developed in Israel for the Day of Atonement (called Yom Kippur). This solemn day of prayer and penitence, still observed by Jewish people in our own time, celebrated the Lord's faithfulness in forgiving the sins of his people—even those sins committed "with a high hand" (i.e., sins committed knowingly and willingly). As described in the book of Leviticus, the Day of Atonement involved two rituals of different origin: the offering of sacrifices for expiating sin, and the "scapegoat," an animal that was "loaded with the sins of the people" then driven into the desert to die. In both these rituals the people of Israel discerned God's power at work to forgive and to forget the sins of his people.

After the destruction of the Jewish temple in A.D. 70, the celebration of the Day of Atonement continued—with the obvious exception that the sacrifices and the ritual of the scapegoat were no longer observed. In their place prayers and poems were said which stressed God's mercy and fidelity despite the faithlessness of his people. In the third and fourth centuries A.D., one of these prayers (actually a poetic hymn) assumed special importance in the celebration of the Day of Atonement. This hymn, called *"Attah Konanta,"* is particularly interesting because it places repentance in the context of a hymn of praise for God's deeds in creation and redemption.

The theology of this hymn suggests that penance is not a clinical procedure by which God plucks shrapnel out of the bodies of wounded people; rather, *penance is a motive for praise and thanksgiving.* God's inevitable reaction to human sin is compassion and mercy; and so, *even sin becomes an occasion for praise,* for "eucharist" (the Greek word, as is well known, literally means "giving thanks"). Some lines from this important Jewish hymn will help illustrate this point:

> In the beginning you created the earth,
> You fashioned the world, made all things,
> You molded all creatures.
> When you gazed at the abyss, the emptiness, the darkness,
> You chased the clouds away and aroused the light.
> From clay you formed your own image and commanded him
>   not to eat of the tree of life. . . .
> Suddenly as a star, a "great father of many nations" shone out
>   of Ur of the Chaldees to light up the darkness (Abraham);
>   and your anger softened when you examined his works:
>   in time of old age you tested his heart. . . .
> You gave him (Abraham) twelve tribes beloved of the Most High;
>   you called them from the womb. . . .
> You consecrated Aaron and his sons, and

> clothed them with the vestments of ministry:
> their sacrifices calmed your anger. . . .

In this hymn, penance is seen as part of the whole history of Israel's creation, election and salvation. The sacrifices offered by the priest Aaron are the signs of Yahweh's passion for people—his intense love, his desire for peace and communion with humankind. Forgiveness is not a gift grudgingly given by a God who would prefer cruelty; rather, *sin, repentance and forgiveness are an intimate part of the history of salvation itself.*

It is Ligier's argument that this hymn, and others like it, in the service for the Day of Atonement, influenced Christian thought about the link between eucharist and forgiveness of sins. Like the Jewish hymn, *"Attah Konanta,"* the Christian eucharistic prayers *place sin and repentance in the context of God's mighty deeds of creation and salvation.* Sin and failure—and sin's reversal through Jesus' sacrifice on the cross—are part of the very process by which God calls people to receive his gifts in human history. And it is this process—God's passionate gift of himself in Christ, given even to sinners—that causes Christians to "make eucharist." If we look closely at the eucharistic prayers used even today, we can see this theme. Here, for instance, is a section from Eucharistic Prayer IV:

> Father, we acknowledge your greatness:
> all your actions show your wisdom and love.
> You formed man in your own likeness
> and set him over the whole world
> to serve you, his creator,
> and to rule over all creatures.
> Even when he disobeyed you and lost your friendship
> you did not abandon him to the power of death,
> but helped all men to seek and find you.
> Again and again you offered a covenant to man,
> and through the prophets taught him to hope for salvation.
> Father, you so loved the world
> that in the fullness of time you sent your only Son. . . .

To a remarkable degree these lines from Eucharistic Prayer IV follow the pattern and themes found in the ancient Jewish poetic hymn for the Day of Atonement. Just as the Jewish hymn celebrates God's loving acceptance of the sacrifices offered by Aaron and his sons, so Prayer IV praises the love with which God accepted the offering of Jesus, who was sent "in the fullness of time."

A word should be said here about the meaning of sacrifice both as used in the Jewish liturgy for the Day of Atonement and as applied to the eucharist by Christian believers. Quite often, the modern view of sacrifice stresses the giving up of something precious, the destruction of something valuable. Catholics used to talk this way about sacrifices during Lent (which often meant "giving up" candy or "giving up" the movies). This view of sacrifice has also affected our attitude toward blood. Blood is a sign of violence and gore, a sign of the destruction and *loss* of life. But in the ancient Jewish view, blood and sacrifice were ways to speak about *presence of life,* not absence and loss. Blood signified the robust presence and power of life itself. Naturally the Jewish people realized that excessive loss of blood could signal the extinction of life, but their primary insight was that *blood makes life present.* When the Hebrews smeared the blood of lambs on their doorposts in the book of Exodus, it was a sign of protection and life, not of destruction and death. The same is true of the ancient Jewish understanding of sacrifice. The important thing about sacrifice was not that something (or someone) got killed, but that a communion of life was established between the people and God. Just as blood meant life, so sacrifice meant communion in life.

It was this ancient Jewish view of blood and sacrifice that influenced the early Christians' understanding of the cross and death of Jesus. Jesus' blood "poured out for many" signified the raw power of life itself present to people, washing them clean, healing them and making them whole. Similarly, Paul calls Jesus our "paschal lamb who has been sacrificed" (1 Cor. 5:7)–not simply because Jesus died violently, but because his death established communion once and for all between human persons and God. According to Paul, the cross is incontestable evidence of reconciliation and of a healed relationship between God and humanity. The death of Jesus, his "sacrifice," inaugurated a new world of possibilities for people; it opened up a path toward peace and pardon "through the blood of the cross" (Colossians 1:20).

If blood means "presence of life" and sacrifice means "communion in life," then we can begin to make better sense of Paul's famous attack on the community meals in the church at Corinth (1 Cor. 11). Catholics have often tried to force Paul's admonitions to the Corinthian community into a full-blown treatise on eucharistic real presence and transubstantiation. But actually, Paul's primary intention is to show the Corinthians that the *meaning* of their community meal (Lord's Supper) is to be found in Jesus' *death*: "As often as you eat this bread and drink the cup, you proclaim the Lord's *death* until he comes" (1 Cor. 11:26). Why *death*? Was Paul just having a particularly morbid day? Maybe—but the more likely interpretation is that Paul wished to show that Jesus' death, his sacrifice, established communion. If the Corinthians were giving themselves over to factions and wrangling, how could this communion of life be revealed in their celebrations of the Lord's Supper? What bothered Paul was not that some of the Corinthians were denying the real presence, but that they were refusing to recognize the body, i.e., they were destroying the church's unity, its communion in life established through Jesus' sacrificial death.

The early Christians perceived the eucharist as sacrifice precisely because it celebrated the presence of life and communion in life. Such a presence and communion could best be symbolized by sharing food and drink around a common table. Sacrifice and meal both pointed to the same reality: the radical unity of persons who ate the same bread and drank from the same cup. Table fellowship, already an important aspect of Jesus' ministry, became the most fitting symbol of the sacrifice that brought Jesus' ministry to completion.

Moreover, just as Jesus' invitation to table fellowship offered people peace, so Christians saw in bread broken and cup shared the signs of reconciliation. Further, just as Jesus' table ministry *challenged* people to accept the message of forgiveness, so the table of Christians continued that challenge. The late biblical scholar, Norman Perrin, once remarked that the table fellowship of Christians became a "symbol of the new kind of relationship made possible by the common acceptance of the challenge" (Perrin, 1967, 107). The table of the Lord's Supper was thus a double challenge: it invited sinners to abandon their rebellion and find peace in eating and drinking; it challenged the virtuous to continue Jesus' mission of reconciliation.

The Jewish tradition of prayer and sacrifice—a tradition of which Jesus himself was a part—thus provides a rich context for understanding the relation between eucharist and forgiveness of sins. We have seen that the Jewish hymn for the Day of Atonement placed sin and repentance in the context of praise for God's mighty deeds in creation and salvation. Despite its destructiveness, sin becomes a motive for praise and thanksgiving, for eucharist. And the same is true for the early Christian interpretations of Jesus' death. Paul puts the matter sharply and succinctly: "For our sake (God) made him to be sin who knew no sin" (2 Cor. 5:21). The very sin that destroyed Jesus in death becomes an occasion for life, praise and thanksgiving. The familiar words of the liturgy for Easter are shocking but true: "O happy fault! O necessary sin of Adam, which gained for us so great a Redeemer!" Jesus' death opened the way to forgiveness, and both death and forgiveness are central to the meaning of the Lord's Supper.

The Early Fathers of the Church

The Fathers of the Church, especially those of the East, also recognized the relation between the Lord's Supper and forgiveness, even though their interpretations of that relation varied. This is refreshing news, since we sometimes think of the Fathers as severe, humorless men who spent their nights dreaming of ways to make Christian life hard for sinners! It would be wearisome to list here the names of all these men along with their respective opinions. But it may be helpful to summarize how these important thinkers and pastors from the early centuries of Christianity regarded the relation of sinners to the eucharist.

1. *A variety of paths to reconciliation.* We have already noticed, especially in the second essay in this volume, that Christians have sought forgiveness in a variety of ways throughout history. It is significant that some of the earliest Christian theologians encouraged that variety. For example, Origen (ca. 185-254), one of the greatest biblical scholars of all time, listed among his remedies for sin such things as almsgiving, forgiving others, converting the sinful, showing charity, disclosing one's sins to a priest, baptism and martyrdom. He also mentions the eucharist as an opportunity for forgiveness. In the West, St. Ambrose of Milan (ca. 339-397) gives a similar list. These lists have more than a quaint antiquarian interest. They reveal something crucial about the pastoral attitude of the Church Fathers. These men were more interested in the unity that results from reconciliation than in a rigid uniformity of penitential discipline. Reconciliation and forgiveness are responses to human need—and those responses can assume a variety of forms.

2. *Development of categories of sin.* At the same time, the Fathers were realists. They acknowledged that some sins are so destructive of a community's life that table fellowship at eucharist becomes impossible. In the writings of the Fathers we can begin to see, therefore, a distinction between those sins which exclude from the common table of eucharist and those that do not. This distinction should not be confused with the later language of theology which spoke of venial and mortal sins. For most of the Fathers, those sins were "deadly" which directly tore at the social fabric of the community itself: things like murder, apostasy and serious sexual irresponsibility (e.g. flagrant and frequent adultery).

72

Sins of this sort demanded at least temporary exclusion from the Lord's Supper not because the eucharist failed to offer forgiveness, but because these sins were like an acid that ate away the very bonds which united believers around the table.

3. *The role of the Spirit in eucharist and forgiveness.* The Fathers of the Church also seem to have paid close attention to the work of the Holy Spirit in the eucharist and in the forgiveness of sins. The Spirit given in baptism is the same Spirit that anointed Jesus for mission, the same Spirit that transforms both the gifts and the people at eucharist into the body of Christ, the same Spirit that forgives sin in Jesus' name. The Fathers stressed the *permanence* of the Spirit in Christian life. Even when a Christian sins, the Spirit does not vanish or evaporate into thin air. The Spirit remains at work in sinful believers, praying in them and moving their hearts toward conversion and reconciliation. Speaking of the Spirit's continuing work in the believer, a Syrian writer with the rather unlikely name of Philoxenus of Mabboug (†523) wrote: "The Holy Spirit which . . . we have received in the water of baptism, has not come to us in such a way that it remains near us at some times and departs at other times. . . . We have become a temple in which he dwells continually. . . . A sin of action or of thought cannot destroy the temple of God. . . . There is no sin which can despoil us of our baptism—neither adultery, nor theft, nor fornication, nor false witness—none except the denial of God and communion with the demons."

Philoxenus' position—one held by other Church Fathers as well—was that sin can never destroy the presence of the Spirit: for without the Spirit repentance itself is impossible, and God never refuses the sinner an opportunity for conversion. The same Spirit works in baptism, in eucharist and in forgiveness. As Philoxenus put it: "If sinners can't approach the mysteries (of the eucharist), *why* and *for whom* were they (the mysteries) given? For as the Lord says, 'This is my body broken *for the remission of sins*.'" Thus, it is not the Spirit that flees before sin, but sin that flees before the Spirit.

In light of the Fathers' emphasis on the work of the Spirit in the sinful believer, it is significant that the prayer of absolution in the new Rite of Penance includes these words: "God, the Father of mercies, through the death and resurrection of his Son, has reconciled the world to himself *and sent the Holy Spirit among us for the forgiveness of sins. . . .* "

The Liturgies of the Eastern Church
The theme of eucharist and forgiveness of sins appears not only in the

writings of the Church Fathers but in the liturgies of both East and West as well. Let us examine some of the evidence for this theme by turning our attention first to the liturgical traditions of the Eastern churches. It will not be necessary for our purposes to list all the examples of eucharistic texts that speak of forgiveness. We will select a few examples that emphasize the connection between the eucharistic offering and the remission of sins.

1. *The offering of incense at the eucharistic liturgy.* Since the Second Vatican Council, the use of incense at Mass is sometimes regarded with suspicion; it seems to represent a hankering after the old ways. People who use incense are sometimes thought of as "effete liturgical snobs" who secretly long for a return to Latin and Gregorian chant. Actually, of course, the use of incense in worship is far older than Christianity. The idea that worship should smell good as well as look good and sound good is ancient. There is something about being human that enjoys finding in worship a festival for the senses. And since the sense of smell is part of being human, Christians through the centuries have not hesitated to make their liturgies "smell" festive as well as look festive.

The natural power of smoke and smell also triggered a symbolic understanding of the use of incense in worship. In that smoky perfume both Jews and Christians perceived a sign of human prayer and God's blessing. Christians therefore used incense frequently when the community gathered to pray at the Liturgy of the Hours. They also used it when the community gathered around the table of the Lord to "make eucharist." The following prayer is taken from the entrance rite of the "Liturgy of St. James," an ancient order for celebrating the eucharist that dates, in its original form, from the fourth and fifth centuries.

> God, you accepted the gifts of Abel, the sacrifices of Noah
> and Abraham, and the incense of Aaron and Zachary. Al-
> though we are sinners, accept from our hand this incense,
> an odor of sweetness. Let it bring about the forgiveness of
> sins for all your people: for you are blessed, and glory is
> yours, together with your only-begotten Son . . .

The natural symbolism of incense (sweetness, rising smoke) signifies both the penitence of believers and the joyful forgiveness promised by God.

The idea of praying for forgiveness at the beginning of the eucharist is echoed even in contemporary liturgical rites. Roman Catholics are familiar (sometimes painfully so) with the penitential rite at the beginning

of Mass. And other Christian communions have similar rituals that introduce the celebration of the Lord's Supper. For example, the revised
Book of Common Prayer (1976) for the Episcopal Church in America
contains two optional penitential orders for this purpose, as well as the
beautiful prayer for purity which may be said just after the celebrant
greets the people:

> Almighty God, unto whom all hearts are open, all desires
> known, and from whom no secrets are hid: Cleanse the
> thoughts of our hearts by the inspiration of thy Holy Spirit,
> that we may perfectly love thee, and worthily magnify thy
> holy Name; through Christ our Lord.

Similarly, the *Worshipbook* (1970), for use in churches of the Presbyter-
ian communion, contains a confession of sin and declaration of pardon
at the beginning of its "Service for the Lord's Day," which includes celebration of the Lord's Supper.

It could be argued, of course, that these rituals of preparation prove
nothing about the power of the eucharist to forgive sin. Indeed, it could
be said that such penitential rites prove just the opposite: forgiveness is
necessary *before* one approaches the Lord's table. Let us, then, look at
some texts that *do* speak explicitly about the role of the eucharist in
forgiving sin.

2. *Petitions of forgiveness within the eucharistic prayer itself.* In the
churches of the East, there developed the custom of praying for the remission of sins—even grave and scandalous ones—*within the eucharistic
prayer itself.* In effect, a kind of prayer of absolution was inserted into
the great prayer of thanksgiving. Here is an example of such a prayer
taken from the "Liturgy of St. James" mentioned earlier: "O God, grant
us peace: pardon and forgive our sins—those done willingly and unwill-
ingly, those done knowingly and unknowingly—whether by word or
thought, whether secretly or openly. . . . "

What is the significance of a prayer like this one? Is it merely a pious
homily about sin and forgiveness thrown into the middle of the eucharistic prayer? Probably not. Those who created this prayer and used it
in worship seem to have sensed that since the eucharistic is a sacrifice
(a communion of life), it cancels the guilt of sin and opens up a new
reconciled relation between believers and God. In the minds of the people who shaped this prayer, the eucharist was not a reward for the strong
and virtuous but healing medicine for the weak and needy.

75

Liturgical scholars like Louis Ligier, whose work has already been mentioned, believe that these prayers of forgiveness within the eucharistic prayer are actually the most ancient examples of absolution in the Christian church—much older than the prayers of absolution associated with either public penance or private penance. This is an important point. It means that the eucharistic prayer was understood not only as a proclamation of God's great deeds in history (creation, election, salvation in Christ), but also as a proclamation of God's forgiveness of sin. The primary focus of the eucharistic prayer was not the consecration of the elements of bread and wine, but the joyful announcement of God's act of reconciling the world to himself in Christ.

3. *Prayers for forgiveness at the beginning of the communion rite.* In a number of Eastern liturgies, then, the eucharistic prayer itself effectively proclaimed the forgiveness of sins. This proclamation was not merely a catechetical device designed to instruct Christians about God's mercy, it was an effective opportunity for them to seek and find reconciliation. Other Eastern liturgies placed similar prayers of forgiveness (absolution) at the beginning of the communion rite. One of these prayers, used by Egyptian Christians who spoke the Coptic language, is very old. It speaks forcefully about the remission of sins granted to those who were about to receive the Lord's body and blood. What follows is a partial translation of that prayer:

> Lord God almighty, you heal our souls, bodies and spirits.
> Through Jesus Christ our Savior, your only-begotten Son,
> you spoke to Peter and said: "You are Peter and upon this
> rock I will build my church and the gates of hell will not
> prevail against it. To you I give the keys of the kingdom of
> heaven: Whatever you bind on earth will be bound in heaven;
> whatever you loose on earth will be loosed in heaven." O
> Good One, Lover of humanity, absolve our brothers through
> your Holy Spirit. God, you take away the sins of the world:
> accept the repentance of your servants . . . and grant them
> remission of their sins. For you are a merciful God, long-
> suffering, compassionate and just. If we have sinned against
> you in word or deed, pardon and forgive us, O Good One,
> Lover of humanity. . . .

The emphatic, almost legalistic, language of this prayer ("You are Peter . . . , whatever you bind. . . . ") should not be overlooked. The prayer is not a warning against sinners who are liable to "make a bad communion"; it is a public offer of absolution and forgiveness. Notice, too, the *communal* language of the prayer. God is asked to forgive *all* who are gathered at the eucharistic table through the power of the Holy Spirit. Furthermore, this prayer does not make categorical distinctions among sinners. For example, the prayer does not say: "Absolve those who are guilty of 'venial' sins, but reject those who have committed 'mortal' sins." Without attempting to classify sinners or sins, the prayer simply asks God to absolve and pardon *all* who approach the eucharist with sincere repentance.

These prayers of forgiveness in the eucharistic liturgies of the East represent, therefore, a genuinely pastoral effort to make the gift of reconciliation as widely available as possible. They acted as invitations, beckoning sinners to discover peace and pardon at the table of the Lord. While some sins, as we have seen, clearly excluded Christians from the eucharist, others were regarded as serious but not deadly. The eucharist itself was offered as a healing medicine to persons who had failed—even seriously—in their Christian responsibility, but who were trying to find their way back to the path of conversion.

The Liturgies of the Western Church

The relation between eucharist and forgiveness of sin can also be found in the liturgical tradition of the Western churches, though perhaps in a less explicit way. Probably the most obvious Western example of prayer for forgiveness in the eucharist occurs in the ritual of preparation for receiving the Lord's body and blood: the Our Father, the prayer that follows it ("Deliver us, O Lord, from every evil. . . . "), the prayer for peace ("Lord Jesus Christ, you said to your apostles, 'I leave you peace. . . . '") and the private prayers said by the priest before he distributes the sacrament.

This cluster of prayers, together with the acclamation "Lamb of God," is actually a small penitential rite that emphasizes the forgiveness offered to Christians through the body and blood of Christ. Although we often do not notice it, some of these prayers explicitly allude to the power of the eucharist to cleanse and heal sinners. Here, for instance, is a portion of one of the private prayers said by the priest before distributing the eucharist to the people: "Lord Jesus Christ, Son of the living God, by the will of the Father and the work of the Holy Spirit, your death brought life to the world. By your holy body and blood free me from all my sins and from every evil. . . . " According to the theology of this prayer, it is the presence of Christ's body and blood that liberates people from sin.

But the most important petition for forgiveness in the eucharistic liturgies of the West is unquestionably the prayer Jesus himself taught, the Our Father. The use of the Lord's Prayer at the celebration of the eucharist goes back to at least the fourth century, perhaps earlier. Two of the prayer's themes—forgiveness and nourishment—made its use at the Lord's Supper seem particularly appropriate. Both bread and forgiveness are life-sustaining realities: the first feeds human hearts and bodies; the second leads sinners into the new world of a reconciled existence.

Even more significant is the point in the liturgy at which the Lord's Prayer is said: communion. Earlier in this essay we noticed that Jesus' preaching and ministry emphasized three elements: the message of the kingdom, the fellowship of the table and the challenge of forgiveness. The kingdom Jesus preached in parable became present in the fellowship of the table, where "sinners and tax-collectors" found an invitation to peace and pardon. In his own person, in the Word, and in the ministry of the table, the kingdom of God was made flesh. And that kingdom was and is nothing less than the ultimate communion of life and love to which all human persons are called.

By praying for the coming of the kingdom in the Lord's Prayer, Christians are actually praying for that communion in life which is born of forgiveness. At the Lord's table both kingdom and forgiveness are made flesh. To share one bread and one cup is to enter into the new covenant of reconciliation established in Jesus' blood. The eucharist is thus the holy sign of feasting in the kingdom of God; it is the festival of reconciliation for sinners.

Summary

This essay has examined the relation between eucharist and forgiveness of sins as expressed in the history and liturgical traditions of the Christian community. We have noted Jesus' invitation to kingdom and table, the influence of Jewish patterns of prayer on the Christian eucharist, the theology of the Church Fathers, and the liturgies of both East and West. What does this history tell us about the ways Christians have sought pardon and reconciliation?

1. It cannot be stressed too often that the history of Christian penance is a history of *variety* and *change*. Historically, the paths to reconciliation have been—and remain—numerous. Christians have sought pardon for sins in ways sacramental and non-sacramental, liturgical and non-liturgical, public and private. History tells us that there is no single, universally valid path to conversion that excludes all other possibilities. The

present essay has tried to show how and why Christians have found in the Lord's Supper a rich source of forgiveness and renewal of life. To say that the eucharist *proclaims* and *accomplishes* the forgiveness of sin is not to deny the effectiveness of other forms of penance, whether public or private. The church's mission of reconciliation in the world is a many-faceted work which draws on a wide range of human experiences. The mission to reconcile sinners is part of the church's larger responsibility of proclaiming the gospel of the kingdom in Word and Sacrament, in preaching and table-fellowship.

2. This history tells us that the eucharist is a reality far richer than academic debates about the moment of consecration or controversies about the real presence. Sometimes we have actually diminished our understanding of the Lord's Supper by being too preoccupied about questions of substance, accident and presence. From time to time we have forgotten that the primary and original purpose of making eucharist is to proclaim God's wonderful deeds with praise and thanksgiving. We have to remember that making eucharist is a verb, not a noun—a proclamation, not a museum of orthodox doctrines. Chief among those wonderful deeds for which we make eucharist is God's forgiveness, his gift of reconciliation through Christ and the Holy Spirit. At the Lord's table we publicly announce that God *remembers* people, i.e., continues to act on their behalf. And when God remembers human sin, he continues to act by forgiving.

3. History reveals that table fellowship, in the ministry of Jesus and in the mission of the Christian people, is a powerfully effective symbol of forgiveness. Table and meal are real symbols of fellowship in faith and love; altar and sacrifice are real symbols of communion in life. Both symbolisms are the same: table/meal and altar/sacrifice point to the same action: God at work in Christ reconciling the world to himself. Both meal and sacrifice have the same purpose: the gathering together of all who believe (of all who *sin*) into the fellowship of the kingdom. Altar and table are invitations to sinners; both offer healing and pardon to people who fail.

4. Finally, history reveals that the eucharist is an *effective* proclamation of forgiveness. This is a point long acknowledged in Christian liturgical tradition, but sometimes forgotten in both theology and pastoral practice. Time and again the prayers contained in the Missal of Paul VI emphasize the relation between eucharist and forgiveness. Here are a

few examples:

> God mercy,
> may this eucharist bring us your divine help,
> *free us from our sins,*
> and prepare us for the birthday of our Savior
> (Third Sunday of Advent)

> Father,
> accept the gifts we offer.
> *By our sharing in this eucharist*
> *free us from sin*
> and help us to look forward in faith
> to the glorious coming of your Son . . .
> (Christmas eve, morning)

> Lord, hear our prayers.
> *By this eucharist free us from sin*
> and keep us faithful to your word. . . .
> (Second Sunday after Christmas)

> Lord, *in sharing this sacrament*
> *may we receive your forgiveness*
> and be brought together in unity and peace. . . .
> (Third Sunday of Lent)

> Lord, *may this eucharist forgive our sins,*
> make us holy,
> and prepare us for the eternal life you promise
> (Wednesday, Third Week of Lent)

Prayers like these are not simply cases of exaggerated language in the liturgy. They are expressions of the Christian community's long-standing tradition that the Lord's Supper is an invitation to pardon and reconciliation. They reflect the same spirit which prompted the bishops at the Council of Trent to remark that the offering of the eucharist brings penitent persons the power of the Lord's cross, a power that cancels even the most enormous sins.

The eucharist, then, continues the ministry begun in Jesus' preaching and in his invitation to table fellowship. Rooted in the Jewish tradition of prayer, praise and sacrifice, the Christian eucharist proclaims the good news of forgiveness. When believers gather to "do the memory" of Jesus, they experience once more the bread and cup of reconciliation.

References

Studies by Father Louis Ligier: Father Ligier's work, referred to in this essay, is largely in French. The relation between Jewish notions of sacrifice, particularly for the Day of Atonement (Yom Kippur), and the Christian understanding of eucharist is studied extensively in his *Péché d'Adam et péché du monde: Bible, Kippur, Eucharistie,* ("Théologie" series, nos. 43, 48; Paris: Aubier, 1960-61). Available in English is Ligier's important article, "The Origins of the Eucharistic Prayer: from the Last Supper to the Eucharist," in *Studia Liturgica* 9 (1973), 161-185.

Jewish Prayer Texts: A useful collection of Jewish liturgical texts in English, with introduction and commentary, may be found in Bernard Martin's *Prayer in Judaism,* New York: Basic Books, Inc., 1968.

CHAPTER SIX

The New Rite of Penance: A Theological Evaluation

Godfrey Diekmann, OSB

In the last twenty years there has been an avalanche of books, of historical and theological articles, and of related materials on the sacrament of penance. The very abundance of this material has made it difficult to assimilate and to synthesize. Thus, when the new Rite of Penance was rather late in appearing, it was certainly not because insufficient research had been done. Although the research was massive, consensus about its meaning among theologians was not easily forthcoming. I do not know of a single theologian in the field who is entirely satisfied with the new rite. Conflicting interpretations of the historical and theological facts which surround the development of penance in the Christian church have made such a consensus nearly impossible.

An additional reason that has made consensus about the new rite difficult stems from a major shift from deductive to inductive theology since the Second Vatican Council. Formerly the matter was quite easy. Certain declarations, such as those from the Council of Trent, were taken as a sufficient theological starting point; from these were deduced logical conclusions about what is essential, what is legitimate, what is permissible. The inductive method, on the other hand, is more sensitive to the theological changes and developments which have occurred in history. It takes into account the recent scholarly investigations of scripture, as well as the historical development of doctrine itself. It is generally recognized today that a council like Trent was deficient in its knowledge of the historical development in previous Christian centuries.

A third factor has also contributed to this lack of consensus among theologians. The Second Vatican Council made it clear that the theology and practice of the Eastern churches must be taken into account and accorded equal status and equal import with the traditions of the West. Thus the Council's *Decree on Ecumenism* (#17) says: "This sacred synod declares that the heritage of spirituality and liturgy, of discipline and theology in the various Eastern churches belongs to the full catholic and apostolic character of the church." The Eastern churches not only possess true sacraments, but in the case of "physical or moral necessity," Catholics may request the sacraments of penance, eucharist and anointing of the sick from ministers of other churches who possess valid sacraments (see the *Decree on the Eastern Churches,* #27). All of this should make people of the Western and, especially the Roman Catholic tradition, much more circumspect about asserting what "may" or "may not" be done in the celebration of the sacraments.

Some examples of this last point may be useful. Take the matter of "integral confession," for example. Trent required that penitents individually and privately confess serious sins according to number and species. This, Trent declared, is of divine law. Yet it is clear even from our own Western tradition that such was not always the case. And it is certainly clear that up to the present in the Eastern Orthodox churches, such "integral confession" is not demanded; indeed, public communal confession and absolution are preferred to "private confession."

Or take the example of the formula of absolution. Trent insisted on the declarative form of absolution ("I absolve you") because of the "judicial nature" of the sacrament. For well over a thousand years in the West, however, there was only the deprecatory form, a prayer asking God's forgiveness (e.g., "May almighty God have mercy, forgive . . ., etc.). And this deprecatory form is still the only form of absolution in all the Eastern churches.

Finally, take the example of confessing sin to lay persons. In the West this practice certainly existed, even if its "sacramental efficacy" is disputed. In the East, however, for many centuries confession was made to monks who were considered "spiritual men." Sometimes these monk-confessors, laymen, were considered preferable to priests. We should not forget that scripture itself recommends "confession to one another" in order to obtain forgiveness from persons whom we have injured or offended. Never once does scripture require confession to the church's ministers. I am not drawing conclusions here; I am simply asking that these facts be kept in mind.

Variety and Change

Let us return to the question of penance, and its theological interpretation, in the West. When we look at the history of theology, we are astonished by the many, often mutually contradictory, theological opinions concerning the sacraments. This is especially true during the medieval period, the period of scholasticism. For approximately the first six hundred years of the church's life, the process of dealing with sinners was called "penance," and *penance* was stressed. Indeed, the doing of penance was normally required before absolution was granted; and absolution was available only once during a lifetime.

But as time went on, the emphasis on penance gave way to a stress on *confession*. Popularly, the sacrament is still called that: "confession." The introduction of private confession and repeatable absolution contributed to this shift of emphasis. In theologically sophisticated scholastic circles, arguments centered around items like contrition and absolution. Historically, then, we can notice three different emphases surrounding the sacrament of reconciliation: penance, confession and absolution. All these terms, however, are but partial ones which describe only a part of the total process of reconciliation. For reconciliation is a *process,* one which involves all those phases of penance, contrition and absolution.

The shift of terminology—from "confession" to "reconciliation" as the appropriate name for the sacrament—is not accidental. Reconciliation is the term which best conveys the sense of the Greek biblical term *metanoia*. This term is a comprehensive one; its primary emphasis is the mystery of God's love for humanity manifested in his converting the heart of the sinner, forgiving sins. In fact, reconciliation, forgiveness of sins, can be said to describe the total happening of God's covenant relation to humankind. Paul's thought in 2 Corinthians 5:19 suggests this: God was in Christ reconciling the world to himself and entrusting to us the message of reconciliation. Reconciliation is a total ongoing process which cannot be limited exclusively to what we traditionally call the "seven sacraments." Sin means alienation from God, the disjointing of our loving relationship to God. This radical alienation is, in turn, manifested in our loss of love relationships with others. Moreover, the alienation that is sin is a fundamental fact of human existence; the weakness of sin continues. And since sin continues, so must *metanoia,* conversion and reconciliation. It is clear, then, that *metanoia* is a fundamental Christian imperative and not simply a "change in one's attitude of mind." *Metanoia* does not consist primarily in the "acts of the penitent" but in God's work. The initiative for reconciliation belongs to God, who effects conversion and change in human lives. *Metanoia* is, therefore, man's grateful acknowledgment that it is not we who first loved God, but God who first loved us. Man's response, his "change of heart," consists in the acceptance of that forgiving love. Even the so-called "acts of the penitent" are, when all is said and done, the sacramental beginning of God's gift of reconciliation. Confession itself, biblically speaking, is much broader than a mere listing of sins—the latter itself is genuine only if it is a part of the basic human response to God's mercy. *Confitemini Domino quoniam bonus*: Let us confess, praise, give thanks to God for he is good.

The biblical sense of "confession" as grateful praise and acknowledgment of God's forgiving love makes it clear why we can "celebrate" penance. What we are really celebrating is reconciliation, God's initiative in converting the heart, forgiving sin and inviting us back to communion with the church. It is significant that the story of the prodigal son contains a feast, a celebration.

Here, too, we find ample confirmation of what scripture scholars, theologians and psychologists have been telling us so insistently in recent years. What we call "mortal sin," a basic deep-rooted alienation from God, is likely a much rarer occurrence than we have been accustomed to believe. In any event, it doesn't make scriptural or psychological sense to treat it chiefly as an *external act.*

Moreover, if reconciliation is the continuous operation of God's forgiving love, then it seriously distorts and limits our understanding of that redemptive compassion of God to stress too exclusively the fourth of the seven sacraments as if there, and there alone, God reconciles. Scripture, theology and history clearly teach that there are other sacraments of reconciliation: baptism, eucharist, anointing of the sick. In the Creed, for example, we confess "one baptism for the remission of sins." And both scripture and tradition teach that baptism forgives sin precisely because it is God's way of initiating people into the community of God's family, into the eucharistic community. Baptism necessarily has eucharistic significance. Furthermore, the eucharist itself forgives sin—and not just "accidentally" but legitimately. This is a truth almost forgotten until recent years and it is still disputed by some. Yet, according to Romans 3:25, Jesus became the "expiation" for man's sins by his blood, by his death on the cross. In the eucharist we thank and praise God for the reconciliation once and for all effected in Christ's saving death. Through the eucharistic celebration the church itself becomes a reconciled fellowship. It is not an exaggeration to say that the eucharist is thus the chief and primal sacrament of ecclesial reconciliation; communion is the sign of the fellowship that is achieved. We receive the blood poured out for many for the forgiveness of sins.

This view was certainly supported by St. Thomas Aquinas. He noted that the sacrament has the power to remit all sins and that it derives this power from the passion of Christ, the source and cause of all forgiveness in the church. Trent said much the same thing when dealing with the expiatory value of the Lord's Supper. The eucharist is not another crucifixion, but it does apply the efficacy of the cross—and this application means the forgiveness of all sins, "even the most serious," committed after baptism. Did not the Second Vatican Council say as much, too, when it described the eucharist as the "source and summit" of all grace?

This, of course, raises another question: if communion can itself forgive sin, then is confession before communion necessary? In dealing with this question we need to remember that the Council of Trent was the first to introduce, authoritatively, the practice of the necessity of confessing mortal sins before the reception of communion for Christians of the West. That Trent made such a disciplinary decision is understandable in light of the history of the sacrament of penance in the West. The Fourth Lateran Council (1215) gave us the obligation of regular annual confession of mortal sins—and from that time on, the discussion of "obligation" received ever more constant attention. Still, the discussion was by no means settled at the time of Trent. Trent declared and commanded, but studiously refrained from saying that the "obligation" of confessing was of divine institution. Trent announced a *discipline*; it did not provide a theological resolution to the question. Nor did Trent say explicitly that it would be grievously sinful not to so confess, even though that may have been the conviction of a majority of the Fathers at the council.

As far as the eucharist itself is concerned, however, the mind of Trent is beyond dispute: the eucharist itself applies the reconciling efficacy of Christ's cross to all sins, even the most serious. Whatever else may follow from this, it would seem pastorally imperative to highlight in catechesis as well as in celebration those several reconciling features of the eucharist. For the eucharist is the most important sacrament for the forgiveness of sins. To restore the fullness of the eucharistic assembly—that is always the goal of reconciliation. Even though it has been customary to regard penance as a kind of "second baptism," it would be pastorally more advantageous to stress the relation between penance and *eucharist*. If penance is urged in its relation to the eucharist, there is less likelihood that it will be regarded as "private soul therapy." For the orientation of penance to eucharistic fellowship with the community is obviously *social*.

In addition to baptism and eucharist, the anointing of the sick is also a sacrament of reconciliation and forgiveness. "And if he has committed sins, he will be forgiven" (James 5:15).

But it is not only these three sacraments which offer the Christian reconciliation. The Bible makes clear that *metanoia* is a continuous and never-ending life process. Human beings are always both just and unjust, virtuous and sinful. This is true not only of individuals but of the entire Christian community. The Second Vatican Council did not hesitate to say that the church is "holy, yet always in need of reform." Daily life itself is part of the sacramental process of reconciliation. How then did we come to emphasize so onesidedly the sacrament of penance (meaning "confession") as the almost exclusive opportunity for forgiveness?

One reason for this can be found in the scholastic sacramental debates of the medieval period. With Peter Lombard (†1160), we have one of the first attempts to establish the number of sacraments instituted by Christ at seven. The fourth of these was, as is well-known, the sacrament of penance for the remission of sins. In short, *one particular manner* of reconciling sinners became highlighted. Earlier there were many manners of reconciliation, including other sacraments. By the end of the twelfth century, however, the earlier history of penance and reconciliation was largely ignored in favor of private penance ("confession"). It was this private form of penance that Lombard had in mind when he listed the sacrament as one of the seven. While the listing of seven sacraments did help to clarify certain theological issues, it also resulted in a narrowing and impoverishment of the forms of reconciliation available to Christians in the West.

In our own day, private penance as an *exclusive* form of seeking forgiveness and reconciliation is being questioned, especially by those Christians most dedicated to a life of holiness. The "shopping list" of weekly confession no longer seems to cope with the great social needs of the human family. Indeed, private confession almost seems to be a cop-out in the face of pressing social concerns for reconciliation. It claims to provide one with a "clean slate," even when he knows that, socially, nobody's slate is clean. As a result, the sign of reconciliation is not a genuine sign; frequently, it encourages complacency. Instead of taking away guilt it takes away the sense of social responsibility and dulls the truly human conscience.

It cannot be denied that the traditional form of private penance was essentially "sacred therapy for the individual conscience" and historically derived from the practice of private spiritual guidance for Irish monks. In the minds of many devout Christians, a dichotomy arose between the *private* form of the sacrament's celebration and the *social responsibility* for reconciliation with *all* others which is incumbent on Christians. True reconciliation can never be a private affair accomplished in secret; its very nature is social, public, communal.

These factors need to be kept in mind as we contemplate the declining frequency of sacramental penance among Catholics today. In the past, the question was often presented in terms of *necessary* confession for mortal sins and *devotional* confession for venial sins. Since in our day many consider "mortal sin" (radical alienation from God) rare, does this mean that the "confession of devotion" or the confession for "venial sins" has no place? After all, why kill a mosquito with a sledge hammer? Why invoke the sacramental "arsenal" of penance for slight misdemeanors and delinquencies?

We can approach this issue pastorally if we keep two points in mind: first, that mortal sin, as basic disorientation, may be infrequent; and, secondly, that reconciliation is a constant, never-ending need for all Christians. Since Christians are always both "just" and "sinful," it may be that the sacrament of reconciliation, even if not "necessary" for mortal sin, can become a most useful pastoral means for articulating more extensively and expansively the public recognition of our deeply experienced need for God's intervention of forgiving mercy. It can become the honest, deeply willed affirmation of who we are and who God is—a powerful motivation for achieving a fully human (i.e., a *Christian*) conscience.

The present state of the sacrament of penance in the church's history does not, therefore, justify our becoming prophets of gloom. Consider the following points:

1. If the decrease of frequency in penance is due to a decrease in our sense of God and of sin, then some concern is appropriate. But the fact that fewer people go to "confession" does not necessarily imply a loss of reverence for God or for the things of God. If it is any comfort, history does teach that other eras were much worse off than we. From about the fourth to the ninth centuries, the sacrament of penance was usually postponed to the death bed. This postponement was virtually the "official line"; it was actually encouraged by some church leaders. Moreover, as we have seen, public penance could be received no more than once in a lifetime. Thus, for a number of centuries, there were doubtless many Christians who never received the sacrament of penance at all. Significantly, when the reform of public penance finally did come about, it came not from the "top" but from the grass-roots experience of Celtic piety. There were several centuries of painful transition, of controversy— and Christian lay persons found themselves caught in the middle of it. Ultimately it was the laity that opted, massively, for the Celtic model of more frequent and private confession and absolution—despite opposition from synods and bishops.

2. Our own era is characterized by brutality and inhumanity on a monstrous scale. Yet, as never before have so many persons of good will been so deeply concerned about global injustices, about cynicism in politics, about injustice to the poor, about the horror of war, about the human rights of all peoples, about stewardship, about our ecological responsibility for this earth. Never before have so many been aware that "private sin" is a contradiction in terms. The conscious need and stance

of reconciliation in broadest terms seems to be more keenly felt by more Christians today than when the practice of multiple "private confessions" was still taken for granted. The "decline" in penance may actually signal a more mature and more responsible approach to the enormous social problems our world faces today.

In conclusion, I would venture to point out four issues which, in light of scripture and the history of sacramental penance, deserve more than casual attention in the work of pastoral renewal.

1. The sacrament of penance cannot be renewed except in the broader context of community renewal. Baptism and eucharist are the two basic and most important sacraments of reconciliation—and both of them have as primary objectives the upbuilding of the Christian community. Can penance have any other purpose? The people of God have a God-given inalienable right to experience a community of loving concern. It seems to follow with absolute logic that our chief means of restoring the sacrament of reconciliation to its proper role is the prior restoration of the Sunday eucharistic liturgy as the primal sacrament of mutual reconciliation, as the regular experience of becoming one body because we eat the one bread. It has been a chief weakness of the theology that emanated from both Thomas and Trent that the *ecclesial* dimension of penance has received insufficient attention. The earlier Fathers of the Church possessed a stronger sense of the social character of reconciliation. Jerome said: "God does not restore a member to health until all the members have wept for him." Ambrose expressed similar sentiments. The formula of absolution in the new Rite of Penance seeks to remind us of the role of the entire community in the process of penance when it says: "God the Father of mercies, through the death and resurrection of his Son, has reconciled the world to himself and sent the Holy Spirit among us for the forgiveness of sins; *through the ministry of the Church may God give you pardon and peace.* . . . "This part of the absolution prayer beautifully expresses the intercessory power of the *whole church*—and it is perhaps unfortunate that the decision was made to keep the declarative 'and I absolve you from your sins' at the very end of the formula. For the full absolution formula is the *entire prayer,* not just the words "I absolve you. . . . "

2. We also need to restore the role of the Holy Spirit in our sacramental thinking. Lambert Beauduin said as early as 1914, the Spirit is more than a footnote in the history of salvation. On Easter evening Jesus said: "Receive the Holy Spirit; whose sins you shall forgive, they are forgiven. . . . " Indeed, every sacrament could in fact be described as the action of Christ in our midst whereby he continues to send his Spirit for the upbuilding

of the church into a community of faith and love to the glory of the Father. And this sending of the Spirit was signified, in earliest Christianity, in all the sacraments by the laying on of hands. This laying on of hands was central and common to *all* the sacraments, and it was accompanied by prayer to specify the precise purpose for which we pray for the coming of the Spirit. One could even say that the history of penance during the first 800 years of the church's life was a history of the laying on of hands for the sending of the Spirit. A respectable exegetical case can in fact be made that in 1 Timothy 5:22 ("Do not be hasty in the laying on of hands"), the reference is to penance, not ordination. It was only after the scholastic period, with its stress on contrition and absolution, that the laying on of hands was thought of as unnecessary in the rite of penance. Charles Borromeo tried to restore it in the sixteenth century, but at the same time he seems to have been responsible for the confessional grill (for female penitents, at least). This made the gesture of imposing hands virtually impossible. In any event, it is my conviction that a chief feature of all present-day reforms in the sacramental rites is the restoration to prominence of the laying on of hands as a conferring of the Spirit. It is up to us to realize how important this gesture is—for it will help restore a proper understanding of the Spirit's role in reconciliation. Restoration of the gesture of imposing hands also has profound ecumenical significance. For a long time the Eastern churches have accused us in the West of neglecting the role of the Holy Spirit. With the restoration of the imposition of hands in the new Rite of Penance, we have an opportunity to overcome some of that neglect. Jesus himself healed persons by bodily touching—and the healing church is one who touches man as if to say "Jesus cares; I care; Receive the Holy Spirit for the forgiveness of your sins."

3. Pluralism is needed. For centuries the sacrament of penance was a Procrustean bed. The time came when more and more people concluded that it didn't fit them, so they refused to lie down in it. Our history of penance is a history of changes, major ones—but these changes followed each other successfully in successive periods of centuries. Perhaps the time has come when our needs are such that variety must be available simultaneously. I am not referring merely to the large choice of prayers and ceremonies now fortunately available in the new Rite of Penance. Certainly it is our pastoral task to use these options wisely. But more weighty instances of variety come to mind. Communal services of penance are certainly valuable, but not to the total exclusion of the so-called "private confession" in which there is an unhurried dialogue between penitent and priest and in which words of advice and consolation can

be spoken. I have always felt uneasy during communal confession services in which the penitents tell their sins and the priest immediately gives absolution without another word. The dialogue between penitent and priest is, after all, part of the ministry of healing. Many persons come to the sacrament wanting to hear a human word of comfort and guidance as a sacramental sign of God's personal love. The "give and take" of "private confession" had its origin, it must be remembered, not in a divine command or in ecclesiastical legislation but in the instinctive personal needs of the people of God. And whatever its historical inadequacies may be, the practice remains a valuable one for many Christians. Pluralism demands both a respect for past heritage and an openness to future change.

4. Finally it is my strong conviction that one of the chief lessons taught by the history of all the sacraments, including penance, is the danger of reductionism. In the case of penance the danger is to reduce God's merciful action in several sacraments (and indeed, in *all* of Christian life) to his forgiving of sins in the fourth item of the "sacramental system." And within that fourth item, reductionism further tends to restrict the significance of the sacrament to the "essential" words of absolution ("I absolve you"). Reductionism is infatuation with the "barest minimum for validity." This has probably done more to impoverish penance than any other single factor. For by reducing the sacrament to the "essential words of absolution," we have seriously disregarded the role of the Spirit and of the entire praying community in the process of reconciliation. The result has been a mechanistic and quasi-magical preoccupation with the effect of the absolution formula.

Our catechesis of the new Rite of Penance must therefore be expanded. The prayer of absolution in the new rite is a good place to begin: it stresses the paschal mystery, the role of the Holy Spirit in forgiveness, the ministry of the entire church—and it does this in the context of a significant sacramental gesture, the laying on of hands. Starting from this prayer, it may be possible to help restore the sacrament of penance to a state of normalcy by pointing out its relation to reconciliation in daily life, as well as its relation to our baptismal dignity and to the Sunday eucharist. With dedicated effort, it may be possible to transform penance from "private spiritual therapy" to a conscious and deliberate sharing in the reconciliation of *all* human beings in the world, and to a grateful re-covenanting with Jesus, Savior of the world. For the sacrament of reconciliation belongs to that worship and work which we are privileged to perform through Jesus Christ in the Holy Spirit to the glory of the Father.

CHAPTER SEVEN

The New Rite of Penance:
Its Value for Religious Education

Cora Marie Dubitsky
Nathan Mitchell, OSB

The Changing Environment of Christian Education

In his *Philosophical Analysis and Education*, author John Wilson describes three classes of learners.[1] To the first group, a very small one, belong those people who have an aptitude for scholarly research. Scholars, Wilson suggests, love to pore over documents, ferret out hidden relationships and fine details, and to make balanced judgments based on an extensive knowledge of their field. For the scholar, the pursuit of knowledge is valuable for its own sake, even if the results have no direct application to the ordinary affairs of daily life. A second group of learners are the "intellectually curious," those highly motivated persons who enjoy mental puzzles and who like to "explore things on their own." A third class of learners—Wilson calls them the "vast majority"—are interested only in topics which have a direct bearing on everyday life. Although Wilson's categories of learners may become artificial if pressed too far, they do shed some light on the challenge faced by religious educators at the parish level. The phenomenon of *pluralism,* widely noticed today by social analysts, pastors and theologians, affects the parish environment as much as it does the university classroom or the august chambers of the United States Senate.

Rather predictably, the social and economic pluralism of our culture is reflected in the changing textures of parish life. Religious educators find that they must deal with a variety of learners at the parochial level: "scholars" (persons with a high degree of professional skill and intellectual sophistication); the "intellectually curious" (people who are eager to know more about Christian life in a post-conciliar era); and parishioners (the "majority"?) who seek practical advice about common human problems of love or marriage, family planning, the education of children, growth in the life of faith, prayer and conversion. Moreover, in many places across the country, the demise of familiar educational institutions (e.g., the parish grade school) has intensified the quest for programs which will reach not only to children but parents and other adults as well. Pleas for "adult education," "centers for continuing formation in Christian life," and "centers for pastoral ministry" are commonplace. Gradually, the church is awakening to the need for *an expanding view of ministry* (no longer limited to ordained persons); for *a deeper sensitivity to educational diversity* at the parish level (a recognition of the impact of social and economic conditions on the way people approach the task of learning); and for *renewed attention to the adult believer* in a world where Christian values must compete on the open market for both respectability and allegiance. In short, the rather insulated educational environment of pre-conciliar Catholicism has vanished. Christians are forced to deal with a plurality of competing values, conflicting ideologies and confusing choices.

It is true, of course, that Christians have faced pluralistic situations before in their history. The pages of the New Testament are littered with the remnants of conflict and controversy about how Christians should go about the task of living for the kingdom in unfriendly social environments. Many scholars would agree that Matthew's gospel, for instance, was written for a community in crisis—and that the crisis was provoked not only by the external pressure of persecution but by internal dissensions in the church as well. Thus Matthew hints darkly that there are members of the community who "do not understand" the Word and thus lack true faith (Matthew 13:19: "When any one hears the word of the kingdom and does not understand it, the evil one comes and snatches away what is sown in his heart"). He also complains about the presence of false teachers and prophets who "lead others astray" (Matthew 24:11: "And many false prophets will arise and lead many astray"). External pressure and internal rupture: these were problems familiar to Matthew and they are familiar to us as well. Matthew's emphasis on fidelity to the *words* of Jesus, as handed on by qualified teachers, is part of his solution to pluralism both inside and outside the church he served.

Today, obviously, the pressures and the ruptures are different. Although Catholics in America have faced subtle (and not-so-subtle) discrimination in the past, their social respectability is no longer seriously challenged. As many commentators have pointed out, the election of John Kennedy to the presidency in 1960 "proved" that one could be simultaneously a faithful Catholic and a loyal American. The struggling immigrant church of the nineteenth century was gradually transformed into a familiar piece of the American landscape. There is growing recognition today, however, that this domestication of the church in America has been costly. By becoming an integral part of the American scene, the church has lost some of its former freedom to voice concern as a critic of the conventional social order. The price of acceptance has meant the diminishment of prophetic freedom. Like other large organizations, the church finds itself with debts to pay—the price of its respectability—and this indebtedness sometimes cripples the community's effort to speak out effectively on the salient social and moral issues of our time.

All these elements—the changing shape of parish life, the diversity of "learners" at the parochial level, the high price paid for Catholic respectability in America—have contributed to the changing environment of Christian education. This essay seeks to explore the impact of this changing educational environment on a specific issue: the new rite of reconciliation. More especially, it seeks to evaluate the language, content and structure of the new rite with a view to their usefulness in a program of religious education at the parish level.

The Language and Content of the "Introduction" to the New Rite of Penance

Anyone who writes, from the frightened freshman in "English Comp 101" to the professional essayist, knows how important the audience is to the writer. Precision, clarity and order of ideas, imaginativeness, style —all contribute to the art of writing and to the interest of the reader. Boring writing makes for boring reading—and boring reading makes for swift loss of interest, even if the topic is momentous. This truism is complicated today by the fact that Americans seem less interested than ever before in the arts of reading and writing. As Edwin Newman has argued, we Americans seem possessed of an impulse to put English to death, unobtrusively yet effectively. Like some of our bodies, our language has grown "fat," shapeless and imprecise. We experience enormous difficulty in saying what we mean. A good example may be seen in what Peter Farb calls the "elaborate euphemism": the grand circumlocution that prefers to call bombs "retaliative devices" and prefers to call injustice "profound cognitive dissonance generated by unequal economic opportunity." Governments are masters of the elaborate euphemism. Nothing is so sure as death and taxes, yet death has become "a cumulative statistic relative to the mortality rate," while taxes (everyone knows) are actually "internal revenue."

My point here is that language—its use and abuse—shapes human perception and human imagination. Language not only *informs,* it also *performs* and, if it is not used wisely, it can *deform* both reader and writer. Ecclesiastical documents are just as subject to the fortunes of language, at the mercy of a writer's skill (or the lack of it). This is one reason, I suspect, why ecclesiastical documents often have an impact on the public that is quite contrary to the intentions of the persons who produced them. Take, for example, the Vatican's *Declaration on Sexual Ethics* (December 29, 1975). The debate and disappointment inspired by this document were not due solely to its theological approach to human sexuality. They were due, as well, to the tone, style, and language of the *Declaration* itself. Within the first section of the *Declaration* we are warned, for instance, that "In the present period, the corruption of morals has increased and one of the most serious indications of this corruption is the unbridled exaltation of sex."[2] Notice the aura created by the language of this passage: the times are evil, faithless, "corrupt" and therefore dangerous. As information, such language is trivial (*when,* after all, were the times *not* "corrupt"?). As exhortation, such language is infinitely wearisome (it strikes one as another frantic effort to cry "Wolf!").

One does not have to accept my exegesis of the passage from the *Declaration on Sexual Ethics* to concur with the point being made here: language projects an aura, an atmosphere of its own that can either beguile or repel us. The negative, accusing language of the Vatican *Declaration,* the admonitions against "licentious hedonism" and "relaxation of morals," have one predictable result: the reader quickly loses interest, grows impatient and stops reading. This is unfortunate because, in point of fact, the document has some valuable things to say about the experience of human sexuality in the light of Christian faith. It stresses, for instance, the inalienable dignity of the human person and calls for sensitivity to the psycho-sexual development of individuals. Valuable insights can be lost, however, when readers are given the initial impression that they are about to be upbraided, admonished, scolded or attacked. Readers can be given the impression that sexuality is not a gift to be joyfully accepted and cherished, but a threatening danger that swiftly leads down the road to "hedonism" and "corruption."

Most religious educators would probably agree with Avery Dulles' assessment of the purpose of ecclesiastical documents. Dulles writes that such documents are intended "not simply to communicate a content but to do so in a manner that evokes a suitable emotional and practical response on the part of the faithful."[3] Put in a slightly different way, church documents not only intend to *inform,* they also intend to *encourage* and *persuade.* Information, however precise, and theology, however correct, will not necessarily convince a reader that the topic under discussion is important, valuable or worthwhile. That is why, in their pastoral message *To Teach as Jesus Did* (November, 1972), the National Conference of Catholic Bishops described education as "one of the most important ways by which the Church fulfills its commitment to the dignity of the person and the building of community."4 The bishops went on to say: "The educational mission of the Church is an integrated ministry embracing three interlocking dimensions: the message revealed by God (*didache*) which the Church proclaims; fellowship in the life of the Holy Spirit (*koinonia*); service to the Christian community and the entire human community (*diakonia*)."5

The passage just quoted makes it clear the Christian education is something quite different from the dissemination of "ideas and information about God." Religious educators have to be concerned not only with questions of content but with the transmission of personal attitudes, values and conduct. Message (*didache*), fellowship (*koinonia*) and service (*diakonia*) are all directed toward the goal of personal *transformation,* continuing *conversion* in Christ. But conversion of this sort cannot happen unless the symbols communicated to students by the religious educator are powerful enough to awaken the imagination. For the students' task is not merely to "hear" what is proclaimed in the church's message; they must imaginatively *re-create* the message in order to release its power in their own lives. This is why language is such a vital dimension of the learning process. Conventional, prosaic language—even the hallowed language of traditional theology—has little power to stimulate and re-awaken the students' imaginations. Indeed, the constant repetition of familiar religious language can have a boomerang effect: its very familiarity can stifle a student's effort to re-create the message in terms that are personally challenging. Paradoxically, conventional religious language can become a barrier both to learning and to the process of conversion and maturation in faith.

This last point is an important one because it is closely connected with the way the gospels remember Jesus' own "teaching method." Contemporary biblical scholars have noted that, in his proclamation of the kingdom, Jesus seems to have favored use of the *parable.* The parable, moreover, is not simply a colorful device designed to add "epistemological vividness" to a point of teaching; it is, in a genuine sense, an *attack* on traditional religious language. In their original form, the parables forced the hearer to *re-imagine* the whole relationship between God and humanity. For example, the parable of the yeast mixed in the flour (Matthew 13:33) would have forced Jesus' hearers to re-imagine the kingdom not as a towering, grandiose superpower but as a humble, hidden reality buried deep in the domestic affairs of ordinary human beings. The parables thus functioned to prevent people from seeking refuge and safety in comfortable religious formulas. By attacking traditional religious language, Jesus' parables broke through the barriers of conventional piety and challenged people to face the unfamiliar language of kingdom and conversion. Those who genuinely *heard* the parable were faced with the task of re-creating Jesus' message in terms immediately related to their own life-experience. In a word, the parables forced people to *re-imagine* the relation between God and humanity; to *re-create* Jesus' message in terms that were immediate and personal; and to *stop hiding* behind the formulas of conventional religious language.

These remarks may help us evaluate the language and content of the *Introduction* that accompanies the new rite of penance. Like most official church documents, this *Introduction* bristles with scriptural quotations, allusions to patristic literature, and references to traditional theological concepts (sin and grace, contrition and sorrow, confession and satisfaction). For example, within the first five paragraphs of the *Introduction* to the new rite, the reader encounters 35 sentences, 27 footnotes and 9 direct quotations. Apart from Scripture, many of the sources cited are ordinarily inaccessible at the parish level. Moreover, the language of the *Introduction* is constantly interrupted by both full and aborted references, parenthetical comments, and footnote numberings.

It may be argued, of course, that introductory material of the sort just described is intended primarily for scholars, pastors and theologians —that small group of learners who love to "pore over documents and ferret out fine details." Even if this is true, an objection may still be raised. Scholars, too, after all, are faced with the responsibility of assimilating and re-creating the message of Jesus in language and symbols which have the power to re-awaken the torpid Christian imagination. Indeed, it is the theologian's ministry not merely to "unpack" and defend the church's tradition but imaginatively to *re-interpret* that tradition in the changing language of new cultures and new times. Scholars and theologians are vigorous creators, not pensioned curators of quaint ecclesiastical lore.

In our opinion, the *Introduction* to the new rite of penance fails to provoke this essential work of Christian imagination. Its language is precise, predictable, conventional. It cites all the "correct" sources, but does so in a way that strikes the reader as cut-and-dried, abstract and boring. There is little in the *Introduction* that challenges readers to *create their own stories* of sin and sorrow, conversion and reconciliation. Far from "teaching as Jesus did," the introductory material assumes the voice of a tired professor, one who knows his discipline well but is no longer very interested in it.

A few illustrations will be useful at this point. Listen, for instance, to the way the *Introduction* to the new rite describes the sinful condi-

tion of the church: "The members of the Church, however, are exposed
to temptation and unfortunately often fall into sin. As a result, while
Christ, holy, innocent and unstained (Hebrews 7:26), did not know sin
(2 Corinthians 5:21) but came only to atone for the sins of the people
(see Hebrews 2:17), the Church, which includes within itself sinners
and is at the same time holy and always in need of purification, constantly pursues repentance and renewal."6 There is nothing "wrong"
about this passage; in many respects, indeed, it is a good attempt to express the constant dialectic in the church's life between the facts of sin
and failure and the search for holiness. Reading it, one is reminded of the
work of contemporary theologians like Karl Rahner who have grappled
with the same issue: the simultaneous presence of sin and holiness at
the heart of the church's own life.7 It is possible, then, to interpret the
passage just cited as a refreshing admission, in an official document, that
sinners are not "merely tolerated" at the "outer fringes" of the church's
life, but that sinners reveal God's continuing gesture of reconciliation in
a world that needs it badly.

Having said this, however, one is still operating at the level of abstraction. It is one thing to admit, speculatively, that the holy church is also
sinful. It is quite another to come to grips with the confusing, incoher-
ent story of sin in the lives of ordinary mortals. By way of contrast to
the passage from the *Introduction* to the new rite, listen to these lines
from Allen Ginsberg's poem "Howl!":

> I saw the best minds of my generation destroyed
>   by madness, starving hysterical naked . . .
> who passed through universities with radiant cool
>   eyes hallucinating Arkansas and Blake-light tragedy
>   among the scholars of war,
> who were expelled from the academies for crazy & pub-
>   lishing obscene odes on the windows of the skull. . . . 8

In these violent lines Ginsberg fingers the guilty shame and confusion of
America in the mid-fifties—and he indicts a society that permits such
destruction to go unattended, unmourned, unacknowledged. Reading this
passage one hears a bomb detonate at the center of the brain—and one
knows immediately how painful the search for wholeness and humanity
is in a culture grown blind to its own hypocrisy.

Our point here is not that the authors of the *Introduction* to the new
rite should have quoted Allen Ginsberg instead of the Bible or the
Church Fathers, but that Ginsberg's language, shocking and violent as

it is, breaks the barriers of conventional wisdom, forces us to confront
the brutal impact of misery and human waste. The language of "Howl!"
leaves us no escape-hatch. Like the language of parable, it demands that
we re-evaluate our experience, re-imagine our relationship with God and
humanity. Ironically, Ginsberg's "Howl!"–which makes no effort at all
to be "theological"–succeeds in wounding us with a problem that *is*
theological in the deepest sense: the "scholars of war" grow fat in the
"academies," while people who search for some shred of peace are
"starving hysterical naked."

Another illustration. During the past few years, a number of writers
have pointed out that a central value of the new rite of penance consists
in its making available to Christians a *variety* of ways to experience the
grace of reconciliation: *individual* celebration of the sacrament; *communal* celebration with opportunity for personal "confession"; communal
celebration with *general absolution.* As far as it goes, this is true: the re-
forms of the Council have envisioned new possibilities for celebrating
sacramental reconciliation. As a religious educator, however, one has to
be concerned not merely with the *fact* of new possibilities, but with the
way those possibilities are communicated to believers. It is well-known,
for example, that a change in sacramental practice usually reflects a shift
in *ecclesiology,* a shift in our perception of who the church is and how
it advances its mission in the world. Religious educators, then, need to
explore the *ecclesiological assumptions* that support a document like the
Introduction to the new rite. Presumably, a new form of sacramental
celebration will open up new possibilities for experiencing the community called church. Or, to paraphrase the language of *To Teach as Jesus
Did*: a re-creation of Jesus' message (*didache*) should result in a new experience of the church as fellowship (*koinonia*) and service (*diakonia*).

The *Introduction* to the new rite of penance attempts to deal with
this point in Section III, paragraph 8. There we read: *"The whole Church,
as a priestly people, acts in different way in the work of reconciliation
which has been entrusted to it by the Lord.* Not only does the Church
call sinners to repentance by preaching the word of God, but it also
intercedes for them and helps penitents with maternal care and solicitude
to acknowledge and admit their sins and so obtain the mercy of God
who alone can forgive sins."9

The ecclesiology implied by this passage is rather exciting. It envisions
a Christian community where *all* members assume responsibility for the
ministry of reconciliation. It describes a *community of proclaimers* ("call
sinners to repentance by preaching the word"), a *community of interces-
sors* ("intercedes for them"), a *community of caring persons who heal*

("helps penitents . . . with care and solicitude"). Here, it seems, is an ecclesiology that takes seriously the ministerial responsibility of *all* believers who work to reconcile persons, families, churches and nations. Indeed, the ecclesiological vision of the *Introduction* to the new rite, with its emphasis on shared responsibility in the ministry of reconciliation, seems to agree very strongly with the theology of the church outlined in the *Rite of Christian Initiation of Adults.* In the latter document we are told: "The initiation of catechumens takes place step by step in the midst of the community of the faithful. *Together with the catechumens, the faithful* reflect upon the value of the paschal mystery, *renew their own conversion,* and by their example lead the catechumens to obey the Holy Spirit more generously."[10] Here, too, the *entire church* is viewed as a ministering community responsible for the work of conversion.

Unfortunately this exciting ecclesiology is not carried through in the *Introduction* to the new rite of penance. The document seems to back away from a church where *all* share responsibility for reconciliation. What appeared to be a ministry that involves *all* believers is quickly specified as one that belongs, by divine institution, "to the apostles and their successors": "the Church becomes the instrument of the conversion and absolution of the penitent through the ministry entrusted by Christ to the apostles and their successors. . . . The Church exercises the ministry of the sacrament of penance through bishops and presbyters."[11] The notion of the *whole church* as a prayerful community of shared intercession gets lost in a preoccupation with the ministerial role of bishops and presbyters. One is left with the impression that the view of church as a community of *proclamation, intercession* and *healing* has been abandoned in order to re-affirm the role of *ordained* ministers in sacramental absolution.

While no one wants to deny the service of the ordained ministry in the process of reconciliation, it must be remembered that Christian penance is a great deal more than "confession" and "absolution." Without disputing the responsibility of ordained bishops and presbyters to proclaim the word of forgiveness in sacramental penance, one must still avoid confusing *reconciliation* with the "moment of absolution." Like the catechumenate, penance is a *process* that involves distinct stages of conversion, reconciliation and healing in the lives of penitents. These stages cannot be reduced to a single "sacramental moment" presided over by a bishop or presbyter. Such a reduction can result in a "curb service" mentality: penitents "place their order" (confess), "get served" (absolved), and drive happily away. Several centuries of such curb service should be enough to tell us that the results, in terms of deepening Christian conversion, are not entirely satisfactory.

This assessment of the ecclesiological foundations of the *Introduction* to the new rite of penance may appear harsh. It is offered, however, in the hope of broadening our vision of *who* the church is as a community of intercession and *what* ministry might mean in such a church. Vatican Council II challenged us to move away from a church turned in on itself and toward a church that reaches out to the abandoned, the alienated, the lonely and forgotten. Through a ministry of reconciliation that is rooted in the ministerial responsibility of *all* believers, the church can accept this challenge.

The Structure of the New Rites

Some comments on the structure of the new rites of sacramental reconciliation will bring this essay to a conclusion. Here the question can be stated succinctly: does the basic structural format of the new rites support an environment where *values* (as opposed to sheer "information") can be discerned, responded to, and communicated?

In the past few decades a great deal of research has been done on the way students discover values. Some of this research (see Piaget's and Kohlberg's studies of the ways children learn moral values) has had a significant impact on methods of religious education. It may be useful to summarize some results of recent research in order to discover criteria for evaluating the effectiveness of the new rites of sacramental reconciliation.

1. *Anonymous values generate little enthusiasm and a low degree of commitment.* By "anonymous" I mean values that are free-floating, unattached to the concrete lives of human persons. In the context of Christian theology, for example, "grace" is identified as a value—but it remains anonymous unless one learns to explore the graced textures of a specific human life. It does little good to ask people (children *or* adults) to "ask for God's grace" unless one is willing to explore the territory of that grace as it emerges in the personal biographies of believers. As a value, grace is a *story to be told,* not an impersonal object to be admired.

2. *Human trust is the indispensable coefficient of value-learning.* Commitment to value will not automatically result from logical argument or authoritative demonstration. Quite obviously, people can be convinced that something is true without being convinced that it is valuable or worthy of personal investment. Faith-values, especially today, are subject to the same procedures of critical testing as are other values (or pseudo-values) in our culture. And, as Aquinas noted centuries ago, faith begins

only when one is ready *to believe the testimony of another person.* It is not possible to affirm the values of faith unless one can *trust the person* who testifies to those values.

3. *Threatening environments and "pressure tactics" impede the effective assimilation of values.* Teachers who secure "discipline and respect" by constantly resorting to punitive sanctions (physical punishment, humiliating remarks, sarcasm and verbal abuse) lose on the level of value what they gain on the level of "attentiveness." Environments which threaten put students on the defensive, thus making them bored or hostile.

4. Finally, *values may be present in an educational environment as hidden persuaders rather than as explicit themes.* It is fatal for educators to assume that content, however "objective" it may sound, is utterly "value-free." Even when the content of teaching is not explicitly evaluative, teachers communicate values non-verbally. Frank recognition of this point can help teachers become facilitators rather than manipulators.

These four points about the way students discover values have something to tell us about sacramental reconciliation as a "learning situation." While it is true that worship is not the same thing as catechesis, liturgy *is* a powerful teacher. In the liturgical assembly, *all* have something to learn and something to teach. As communal prayer and worship, the sacrament of penance becomes a "teachable moment"—a moment wherein the community is challenged to re-create the message of Jesus in its own life (*didache*) and thus to discover new forms of fellowship (*koinonia*) and service (*diakonia*).

Do the structures of the new rites of penance support an environment where values can be discovered and assimilated? The answer to this question must be an ambiguous yes and no. Structurally, the pattern of all three rites of penance (individual, communal, communal with general absolution) is virtually identical: reception and welcome; proclamation of God's word; confession of sin; proclamation of forgiveness; thanksgiving and praise. This structure has the advantage of permitting dialogue between ministers and people—and it also permits the celebration to be "shaped" according to practical factors like the size of the community; the *architectural space*; the *age* of the participants; and the *number* of ministers available. In short, the liturgical structure is sufficiently flexible to allow for considerable variety in celebration.

These advantages co-exist, however, with some serious disadvantages. Like many of the liturgical reforms inspired by the Council, the new rites of penance tend toward verbosity. It is almost as though the persons who composed the rites felt sin could be eliminated by *talking* it to death. As noted above, however, values are often communicated non-verbally as hidden persuaders rather than as explicit themes. Mere talk about values will not lead persons to embrace them. Modelling values is far more critical than speeches about their worthiness.

If it is true, as I believe, that reconciliation ultimately deals with social values and with the quality of conversion in a community, then our enthusiasm for the new rites of penance needs to be tempered with a bit of practical wisdom. Like reconciliation itself, the transformation of personal values is a *slow process* that demands time, exquisite sensitivity, and life in a community that cares about sinners. However well-planned and well celebrated the new rites of penance may be, I doubt whether they alone can be expected to *create* the kind of environment that promotes the discovery and assimilation of Christian values. Religious educators today agree that value-formation is a task of "continuing evangelization" rather than occasional celebration. Despite centuries of Christian education, we are beginning to acknowledge that many learners in the community remain unevangelized. Value-formation must often take the form of *evangelizing* rather than catechizing or celebrating sacraments. We can hardly expect people to become enthused about "fellowship" and "service" if they have never really *heard* the gospel in the first place.

Notes

1 New York: Humanities Press, 1965.

2 *Declaration on Certain Questions Concerning Social Ethics.* Washington, D.C.: United States Catholic Conference Publications, 1976, p. 3.

3 *Spirit, Faith and Church.* Edited by Avery Dulles et. al. Philadelphia: Fortress Press, 1970, p. 58.

4 Washington, D.C.: United States Catholic Conference Publications, 1973, p. 4.

5 *Ibid.*

6 *Rite of Penance.* p. 2.

7 See his "The Church of Sinners," *Theological Investigations, Volume VI.* Trans. by Karl H. and Boniface Kruger. Baltimore: Helicon Press, 1969, pp. 253-69.

8 *The Norton Anthology of Modern Poetry.* New York: W.W. Norton and Company, 1973, p. 1121.

9 *Rite of Penance,* p. 5. Emphases are those of the authors.

10 *Rite of Christian Initiation of Adults.* Washington, D.C.: United States Catholic Conference Publications, 1974, p. 1. Emphases are those of the authors.

11 *Rite of Penance,* p. 5.

CHAPTER EIGHT

The Rite of Penance/Reconciliation: Christian Existence in a Reconciled Humanity

Colman Grabert, OSB

Introduction

In this essay I intend to say something about the theological meaning of the new rite of penance by identifying and interpreting some of its elements. Since human beings discover what things mean only by interpreting them, my purpose will be to offer an interpretation of Christian existence as "achievement of identity in Christ." I approach this task as a systematic theologian—thus, some comments about the consequences of this approach are in order at the outset of this essay.

Contemporary systematic theology has been strongly influenced by recent developments in the philosophy of language and by investigations of what symbols are and how they function. Language, after all, is one of the principal methods people use to interpret and "make sense" of their world. Indeed, language not only describes this world, it creates and projects a world of its own. As modern philosophers like Paul Ricoeur have shown, this human framework of language deals with ultimate human problems: the origin and end of evil; the burdensome facts of failure and guilt; the ineradicable desire for wholeness and integrity in life. The "language of confession" (the personal avowal of sin and guilt) acts as an interpretative framework for the ritual symbols and gestures used in the sacrament of penance/reconciliation. At the same time, symbols too have the power of speech, even though they speak in nonverbal ways. For symbols are not things but deeds, transactions that "speak" ultimately about the relationship between humanity and the "Holy." In the celebration of penance, language and symbols interact and comment on each other. Hence the full theological meaning of the rite of penance emerges from an interaction between its "language of confession" and its ritual symbols.

Moreover, the ritual and language of penance stand within the larger context of a Christian "system of symbols" (all the rites and beliefs that comprise the Christian confession of faith). In this system of symbols not everything is of equal importance. One can speak of a "hierarchy of doctrines" in Christianity. Some rites, for example, baptism and eucharist, are more central to the community's life than others (e.g., anointing the sick). This means that the rite of penance derives its fullest meaning from the celebration of the eucharist, traditionally the chief symbol of reconciliation and transformation in the community.

With this background in mind we can attempt a theological interpretation of the new rite of penance. The essay falls into three sections. In the first, I hope to show that the meaning of penance/reconciliation as a whole is the disclosure of an "eschatological horizon of hope." By this phrase I mean that the language and symbols of penance intend to project a "reconciled world" where human beings can strive, freely and creatively, to achieve their personal and communal identity. The "world" of reconciliation is a world of hopeful striving, one where radical new beginnings are both plausible and possible. In this world the *church* stands as a primary symbol of all that reconciliation promises: renewal of covenant, unity with the body of Christ, the final fulfillment of holiness. In this world, too, penitents are invited to move from the "opaqueness" which results from the avowal of sin and failure to the transparent light that breaks forth in the thankful confession of God's reconciling action in Jesus Christ.

In the second section of the essay I hope to explore the significance of the interpersonal, communal and social elements of the rite of penance. There it will be necessary to ask: what does reconciliation with the *community* mean? How does the community *mediate* a true Christian identity to penitents in spite of (and perhaps "thanks to" and "beyond") the fact of sin?

The third and final part of the essay will deal with the grace traditionally ascribed to sacramental penance as one of its primary effects. It will be my intention to explore the meaning of grace as "the church achieving its identity in Christ through love."

The Rite of Penance: The Eschatological Horizon of Hope

Sin as radical threat to identity. Paul Ricoeur has argued that a person's avowal of sin (of guilt, failure and defilement) is a *layered* experience that embraces several significant levels of meaning. At its deepest level the admission of sin results in a bizarre sense of personal estrangement. As Ricoeur puts it, the experience of the sinner is "the experience of being oneself but *alienated* from oneself." The sinner regards himself as an incomprehensible puzzle; God becomes hidden and the course of life becomes meaningless.

Other theologians, like Karl Rahner, have made similar assessments

105

of the impact of sin on human experience. Sin, Rahner maintains, is a fierce "No!" to one's radical self, a refusal to acknowledge one's freedom as a responsible human subject. Moreover, since human subjectivity is radically constituted by the mystery of God in creation and grace, sin is, simultaneously, a massive "No!" to God. The result is frightening: a cavernous abyss seems to open up between one's identity as a free human subject and oneself as a rebellious sinner. Thus conceived, sin is equivalent to radical "flight" from oneself; it threatens the identity of a person with dissolution.

Rite of Penance/Rite of Reconciliation. This notion of sin as alienation from oneself may guide our understanding of the rite of penance. As reformed by the Second Vatican Council the rite carries a dual designation: it is both a rite of *penance* and a rite of *reconciliation.* What does this dual designation signify? It would be a misunderstanding, I believe, to suppose that the two parts of this designation refer to discrete elements of the rite—as though "confession" (penance) were opposed to "absolution" (reconciliation) or as though "sinner" (penitent) were opposed to "minister" (reconciler). It is rather the *whole rite* that is simultaneously penitential and reconciliatory.

As "penitential" the rite deals with the experience of sin as "an obstacle to be overcome"; it aims at a personal wholeness that is not yet experienced but is hoped for. Thus the *penitential* dimension of the rite attempts to expose the experience of sin as alienation, as the dizzying flight from oneself. It does this by bringing sin to light in both an *action* (the ritual gestures) and a *story* (the many-layered story of humanity as "Adam" and of Christ as the "Second Adam"). Action and story set the penitent in motion toward that personal wholeness without which alienation (sin) would not have been recognizable in the first place. Paradoxically, the penitential dimension of the rite is already an acknowledgment of the "reconciled" personal integrity for which the penitent longs.

As "reconciliatory," however, the rite thrusts the penitent into a world deeper and larger than the narrow sphere of his personal thirst for integrity. It is significant that the formula of absolution in the new rite does not dwell on the private peccadillos of sinners. Instead, it raises the curtain on a vast cosmic scene of reconciliation wrought by the death and resurrection of Jesus: *"God, the Father of mercies,* by the death and resurrection of His Son, *has reconciled the world* to himself . . . " In this proclamation the penitent's eyes are forced to turn away from preoccupation with self and toward a universe that throbs with new life since it has been washed clean in Jesus' blood. In short,

the formula of absolution confronts the penitent with the powerful eschatological symbol of a *reconciled world,* the agent of which is God,
the Wholly Other. Everything else—reconciliation with the community,
the "juridical judgment" of absolution, the psychological experiences
of forgiveness and pardon—are subordinate to this central symbol of ultimate reconciliation. Penitents are invited to see themselves not as "iso-
lated units of personal wholeness" but as participants in a much larger
pattern: the pattern through which God invites *all* created reality into
loving communion with himself. The symbolism of a reconciled world
reminds one strongly of C.S. Lewis' image of the "cosmic dance," used
so effectively toward the end of his novel *Perelandra*:

The Great Dance does not wait to be perfect until the peoples of the
Low Worlds are gathered into it. We speak not of when it will begin. It
has begun from before always. There was no time when we did not re-
joice before His face as now. The dance which we dance is at the centre
and for the dance all things were made. Blessed be He![1]

In its reconciliatory dimension the new rite of penance invites believers
to regard themselves not as soloists on a barren stage but as dancers in
the "Great Dance" that "has begun from before always." It is this "Great
Dance" that forms the eschatological horizon of hope towards which the
penitent is beckoned.
The function of the term "church." Every liturgical rite implies an
ecclesiology, and the new rite of penance is no exception to this rule.
In its "Decree of Promulgation," its Introduction and its prayer-formulas,
the new rite invites us to look more closely at the mediating function of
the church in the process of reconciliation. Once again the formula of
absolution suggests a starting point for our reflection: *"Through the ministry of the Church,* may God grant you pardon and peace . . . " How
should this mediating ministry of the "church" be understood, especially
in view of the fact that the Introduction to the new rite clearly affirms:
"God . . . alone can forgive sins"?[2]
Significantly, the Introduction insists that the church carries out the
ministry of reconciliation entrusted to it by the Lord through *preaching*
and *baptizing.* "Church" is thus identified as a community solicitous in
calling the faithful to continual conversion and renewal. Its activity is
described by vigorous verbs like "desires," "tries," "urges." The documents which accompany the new rite do not, therefore, use the term
"church" loosely; they use it as a symbol that evokes the ultimate power
of reconciliation, of giftedness, of holiness and of fulness. Seen in this

light, "church" is part of a matrix of eschatological symbols of reconciliation and is joined to other symbols such as the "eschatological bride," the "body of the glorified head, Christ," the "Holy People of God." The church thus becomes something quite different from an "organization" that is controlled by sociological accidents, crusted ideologies, and juridical red tape. It becomes a symbol, real and effective, of the "reconciled world"—a symbol that simultaneously exposes sin (alienation) and invites sinners to the "Great Dance." The historical community called "church" exists under the power and promise of this symbolism; it exists in the hope of a reconciled world and acts for its fulfillment among men and women everywhere.

There is more to be said about how the church functions as "symbol," but for the moment I want to focus attention on the concrete life of the Christian community as it unfolds in history. Sin (alienation) does more than "wound" believers; it also generates a powerful symbolism of the church as *sinful,* as, to use a provocative phrase, the "chaste harlot." This symbolism of sin re-enforces a set of experiences that all Christians can recognize: the church is a "chaste harlot" but also the "spotless bride of Christ"; members of the church are "weak sinners" but also members of a transfigured body joined to Christ the Head; the church is "holy" yet constantly "in need of purification."

These contrasting symbols—and the experiences they evoke—remind us of the dual designation attached to the new rite: the whole rite is simultaneously penitential and reconciliatory. Just as the entire rite of penance is characterized by the tension between a *hoped-for* reconciliation and an *experienced* alienation, so the historical community (church) lives under the same tension as it moves into the future. Designations like "sinful," "weak," "defiled" refer not simply to sinners and penitents; they refer to the *entire church* as a community which discovers itself both as alienated and as constituted in eschatological hope. And it is this symbolism of hope (the cosmic vision of a "reconciled world" announced in the formula of absolution) that empowers the community to *act* so as to overcome its condition of sinful alienation.

In the new rite of penance, therefore, the term "church" functions not only as symbol and as reference to the historical community, it also functions as "Idea" and "limit-concept." Some explanation of these two notions is in order. Paul Ricoeur has used the notion of "Idea," derived from the philosophy of Immanuel Kant, in the sense of a "horizon of meanings," a "creative theme which gives the general drift of its meaning to the community and thus endows it with a bond and a goal."[3] Idea, in this sense, is a supra-personal work to which we may be devoted, in which we participate, indeed, for which we may give our lives in sacrifice. Closely bound to this devotion to an Idea is our participation in all forms of the "We," of friendship and the interpersonal. We may also die for our friends. At such limits of sacrifice, the infinite character of our heart and the "totalizing" form of an Idea emerge clearly. Far from being simply the sum of individuals, communities, societies, or cultures, the Idea is the objective representation of *all* that we most esteem in others and of all that we expect others to confirm in ourselves. Moreover, to the "formal" character of the Idea there corresponds the "material objectivity" of all the cultural works which provide the Idea with density and thickness. They are the "concrete universals" of the abstract Idea, searching out humanity's possibilities.

This rather abstract explanation may be helped by an example. In the past couple of years television novels like *Roots* and *Holocaust* have attracted wide viewing audiences. While both programs mirrored a particular situation or epoch of our past, both transcended, to some extent, a literal reproduction of the past. Both *Roots* and *Holocaust* gave visual density to the Idea of humanity. They did this both by representing, to our astonishment and horror, the utter corruption and alienation of the Idea of humanity in the chimneys of Auschwitz and by representing the Idea of humanity in figures that affirmed life even in the face of death and the demonic.

"Church", too, functions as both an Idea (abstract, formal) and a "cultural network of objects" in which we interact. The architecture of a great cathedral, the theological synthesis of a thinker like Thomas Aquinas, the renewed pastoral hope inspired by the Second Vatican Council, the delight of liturgy well-planned and well-celebrated—all these form that "cultural network of objects" that give specificity and concreteness to the Idea of church.

Another illustration may be given at this point. In the lives of Roman Catholics, the figure of Mary has inspired a kind of "spiritual sub-culture" represented by a rich abundance of art, music, poetry and dogma. Devotional extravagances aside, these aspects of Marian culture have helped people explore more fully the possibility of existence in a community called church. In poems and hymns, drama and devotion, Christians have evoked the figure of Mary in order to discover new ways of belonging to one another and to God. The symbols that cluster around the Mother of Jesus—virginal single-heartedness, fruitful motherhood, receptive hearing that leads to obedience, the ultimate union of all the living—form a cultural network that has helped persons grasp the concrete meaning of church for daily life.

109

Indeed, the symbols of "Mary/Church/Mother of the Living," particularly as they emerge in works of art, express most powerfully the Idea of church as "reborn, reconciled humanity." Devotion to the Idea of church in the "sinless Mother" of a "reborn humanity" provides a way to discover and esteem in *all* persons the transformation (reconciliation) that beckons us beyond the self-estrangement induced by sin. At the same time, personal love for Mary as a human being who is Mother of the Savior has given Christians an opportunity to experience the interpersonal "We" of the church.

There is another area, too, in which the Idea of the church emerges: the sacraments. Like art and architecture, sacraments form part of the church's "cultural network"; they are concrete expressions of the church's life in a particular cultural situation. As such "cultural works" of the church, sacraments are traditionally said to do two things: they "signify" through symbols (meaningful gestures, words and rites), and they are "infallibly effective" (the doctrine of *ex opere operato*). It is this last point especially—that the sacraments are infallibly effective *ex opere operato*—that has produced endless debate among theologians. In the light of the view of church I have proposed here, I would like to suggest that the troublesome phrase, *ex opere operato* derives its significance from the notion that sacraments are "cultural works" of the church. Like all such cultural works (art, architecture, drama, poetry, music, etc.), sacraments "perform" at the level of *meaning*—or, more correctly, they "project a world of meanings" and invite us to enter that world. That is why there are certain irreducible elements of meaning present in each of the sacraments—elements without which the sacraments fail to perform at all. (Traditionally, these irreducible elements have been referred to as "matter" and "form".) By projecting a world of meanings that express the community's ultimate hope for life and freedom, the sacraments speak, perform, accomplish their work. But this world of meanings is nothing less, ultimately, than the world God has reconciled to himself through the blood of Jesus. The phrase *ex opere operato* (in the sense of infallibly effective) simply serves to affirm this fact: as cultural works of the church, the sacraments can and must project the world of meanings derived from God's ultimate gesture of reconciliation in Jesus. That is the reason why the liturgy of sacraments does more than reflect "where the community's at." Liturgy always challenges us by its invitation to move *beyond* our present environment and epoch toward a "new heavens and a new earth," toward an ultimate vision of humanity as graced and reconciled, toward the "Great Dance" that "has begun from before always." As cultural works that express the Idea of the church, sacraments project this *larger* world of reconciled humanity and, at the same time, permit us to participate directly in the interpersonal "We" of the church —the same interpersonal "We" that was manifest in Jesus' unrestricted love for sinners and outcasts, lepers and uglies, the tragic and the tormented.

This exploration of the function of the term "church" in the new rite of penance has emphasized the importance of *symbol* and *Idea* for an understanding of the Christian community. But there is another term which is widely used today by theologians and which can help us explore more fully the meaning of church. I refer to the notion of "limit-concept" as it is discussed by men like Paul Ricoeur and David Tracy. "Limit concept" expresses the effort to preserve, in our concepts and theological terms, the tension which occurs in an eschatological horizon of experience and thinking between "what we can know" and "what constantly escapes our knowledge." As such a limit-concept, "church" must preserve this tension. On the one hand, we can certainly claim objective knowledge of the church; on the other, the church constantly eludes our capacity to capture and dominate it by knowledge and thinking. In New Testament terms, this is the tension between "knowing now what we are" and not knowing "what we will be" (see 1 John 3:2). In its dogmatic constitution *Lumen Gentium,* the Second Vatican Council struggled with this same tension and spoke frequently of the church as "mystery." "Mystery," as it was used in the Council's documents, did not refer to a riddle or puzzle. It was a way of designating a reality whose inexhaustible fulness both "gives itself to be known" and, in that giving, "exceeds the possibilities of our concepts and our conceptual expression." It is this "excess" of reality, this "fullness" of power that gives rise to symbols, to limit-expressions, to parables. At the same time, these symbols and parables structure our world and our psyches, thereby leading us to limit-experiences, experiences that thrust us toward the very edges of language and thought. Paradoxically, the symbols and parables that thrust us toward the edges of language also give us the possibility of *thinking,* the possibility of concepts. The very *limits* of thinking actually help us to think; the very *edges* of language actually help us to speak, to interact with symbols, to tell stories in parable. Seen in this light, our limit-concepts for realities like God and church are not a useless pile of intellectual rubbish. They are, as Paul Ricoeur has said, a legitimate human way for "thinking the *incomprehensible* and *still thinking*."

Ricoeur's reference to wrestling with the "incomprehensible" provides another example of the way Christians have experienced the tension inherent in a "limit-concept." In their language about God as "Trinity," believers have wrestled with the inevitable tension between "what we can know" and "what constantly escapes our knowledge." As a theological concept "Trinity" has nothing to do with mathematics or divine number-games. "Three" and "One" are symbols for God (as are "Father" and "Son") that intend to evoke the combined power of inexhaustible vitality and absolute integrity. As "Three," God is confessed as fullness, unsurpassed abundance, the presence of all possibilities, the inexhaustible shining forth of all that is alive, loving, truthful and beautiful. As "One," God is celebrated as the ground of all personal integrity, as the ultimate communion of all that is, all that loves, all that breathes beauty into a world graced and reconciled. Just as the Council used "mystery" as a way to speak of the limit-concept "church," so Christians have traditionally used "Trinity" in a way to express the limit-concept "God." In both cases the tension between "what we can know" and "what constantly escapes our knowledge" is preserved. In both cases, too, we can grapple with the realities (church, God) only through the evocative power of symbols (Bride, Body, Holy People, Three, One, Father, Son).

This rather extended analysis of the term "church" as symbol, Idea and limit-concept has been necessary in order to examine more precisely the *language* (and the meanings embedded in it) found in the reformed rites of penance/reconciliation. The rite of penance is performed by an *historical community*. The reforms of that rite, too, have been carried out by an historical community through its Councils, its commissions, its conferences. Still, whenever the rite of penance is performed or reformed, it is "the church" who is said to act. Rites are celebrated (and revised) in and under the symbols that disclose *this* historical community as *church*. As Idea and as limit-concept, the term "church" thus becomes a tool by which we understand ourselves as an historical community of persons who sometimes fail, miserably and wretchedly, but who can still claim the title "holy church of God." The incredible irony and paradox is that precisely *as* an historical community of sinners, we *are* the "holy people of God." It is this paradoxical fact that the rite of penance/reconciliation leads us to discover and celebrate. Far from permitting sinners to wallow in a remorseful guilt-trip, the new rite exposes them to their utmost possibility, their possibility of becoming God's holy people. At the same time the rite empowers sinners to move forward toward the eschatological promise of reconciled humanity, whose symbol is the church itself. Similarly, far from providing illusory solutions to human sinfulness (e.g., the reduction of salvation to some sort of community congeniality or the projection of salvation to a numinous realm that offers flight and escape from reality), the rites of penance/reconciliation invite us to realize our identity as "church."

The "opaqueness" of sin and the identity mediated by Christ. I have argued that the dual designation, rite of penance/reconciliation, leads us to an understanding of the sacrament as empowering the penitent to *recognize* sin as alienation and to *avow* that condition *in hope.* Further, I have suggested that the functions of the term "church" as symbol, as idea and as limit-concept empowers the community to deal with a problem that would otherwise remain insoluble. Succinctly put, that problem may be stated like this: how can a community of alienated (sinful) persons *act* in such a way as to overcome its own alienation (sin)? In other words, how can persons estranged from themselves recover their distinctively religious identity in Christ? It is my conviction that such recovery can happen only through belief in the symbols and rites that mediate that identity and only through faith solicited by the gospel of the kingdom.

Earlier in this essay I alluded to the experience of sin as the "dizzying flight from oneself," as the "hiddenness of God," and as "meaninglessness at the core of life." Sin renders persons "opaque" to themselves —it is like looking for oneself in a window and seeing nothing but the bland surface of frosted glass. On the one hand, the experience of sin fills us with a frantic impulse to "explain" ourselves and our behavior, to "justify" error and evil. On the other hand, this attempt is doomed to futility and failure: the more we try to explain and justify, the more clouded and opaque the vision of ourselves becomes. Such explanation and justification do nothing but further the vertiginous flight from oneself.

Eventually, the sinner discovers that he can deal with the *destructive* power of sin only through the *constructive* power of symbols. That is why literature, for example, almost always speaks of sin/alienation through a *symbolic* discourse—e.g., eating of the "forbidden tree" in Genesis; Joseph Conrad's "heart of darkness"; Lady Macbeth's "damned spot." Such symbolism mediates meaning to persons, allowing them to appropriate that meaning and thus to achieve a human identity. For we achieve our identity as human beings by permitting ourselves to be interpreted by the meanings which symbols mediate—whether those symbols are stories (texts), gestures (rites), or parts of a cultural heritage. The text of the Bible, for example, can be approached as information, as a body of archaic literature, or as an archaeological curiosity. But to approach the Bible *in faith* means opening oneself to the "world" projected by the biblical text, allowing oneself to be interpreted by the biblical symbols. Believers approach the text of the Bible not as something to be manipulated and controlled but as a powerful word that creates, shapes and defines life. Faith is not a matter of inviting the Bible into *our* world, but of accepting the Bible's invitation to enter *its* world. One thus achieves identity as a believer by appropriating the meanings mediated by the Bible's symbols and the community's rites ("sacraments"), just as one achieves identity as a human being by assimilating the "ritual repertoire" of a particular culture.

The same process is at work when sinners confront the fact of their alienation, their opaqueness, their "loss of identity." Such alienation and loss can be overcome only if a sinner opens himself to a world of symbols and allows himself to be interpreted by those symbols. Here we can begin to see why the Christian conviction that Jesus is God's *Word* is so central to the experience of sin and reconciliation. In Jesus, God, who is Absolute Mystery, overcomes the irreconcilable distance between himself and human history by uttering a Word. Word is, after all, the most primary form of symbol. As Word, Jesus thus becomes the ultimate symbol of God in the flesh of humanity. That Word addresses us in the text of the Bible, calls us through the proclamation of Jesus' death and resurrection, and releases power (the Holy Spirit) in our hearts. Jesus the Word is revealed as the one in whom all symbols of eschatological hope coalesce, the one upon whom all desires for a reconciled humanity converge, the one by whom the "Great Dance" begins and ends. By opening ourselves to that Word, by permitting ourselves to be interpreted by Jesus, the ultimate symbol of God in human flesh, we discover our true identity and overcome the self-estrangement produced by sin.

The New Rite of Penance: Ritual Interactions

Up to this point I have been concerned to focus attention upon the *language* of the new rite of penance—and upon what that language can tell us about the experiences of sinning, doing penance, and being reconciled. But a rite is more than a language; it is also a thick set of interpersonal, communal and social *interactions*. Here I should like to identify and examine more closely some of those interactions: assembling, avowing sin to a community representative, absolving, reconciling with the community.

Assembling. The first act of the rite is the act of assembling, of coming together from the dispersal of daily life. This assembling for the celebration of penance takes its full meaning from the great calendar assemblies of Sundays, festivals and seasons. There, the purpose of assembling is clear: it is a coming together to appear as "the church," a striving to exist under the eschatological symbols of the church, to act as empowered by those symbols, to recognize and esteem in one another the Idea of the church. The full meaning of the assembly, as a communal and social fact, is disclosed by a calendar which pivots on the Lord's Day, the rhythmic recollection of Easter week by week. *All* Christian assemblies, therefore, are acts of meeting and coming together under the power of that eschatological horizon of hope established by the event of Easter.

Assembling for the rite of penance/reconciliation has no such calendar designation; it is an action that can be done anytime, anywhere. Still, the fact remains that Christians assemble, ultimately, for one reason alone: to gather themselves around the event of Easter, to allow themselves to be interpreted by the symbols of Easter—life overcoming death, hope vanquishing despair, risen existence triumphing over dead bodies. Easter, with its ultimate (eschatological) symbols of hope, forms the inner structure of *all* Christian assemblies. It is for this reason, indeed, that the proclamation and preaching of the Word has become characteristic of any time that Christians gather for prayer, praise or penance. The Word of God discloses and manifests the meaning of the assembly as *church,* as a community gathered in the power of the resurrection. Significantly, the new rite restores the Word to the celebration of the sacrament—not for the purpose of making the scriptures a kind of "list" for the assessment of moral behavior, but for the purpose of disclosing *this assembly* as church, as the Easter-Community.

The act of assembling (even in the somewhat truncated form found in "individual confession") thus discloses and identifies the church as the community of the resurrection. As the same time it provides the context for the interpersonal, communal and social transactions that follow.

Avowing sin to a community representative. For centuries Christians have been asking the question "why should an individual confess sins to another person in the community?" God alone searches the heart and forgives, after all. And besides, it is more important to repent from the heart than to bore people with a list of offenses and misdemeanors. Various defenses of the practice of "confession" (avowing one's sins) have been attempted by theologians. The very embarrassment of confession, some have argued, is humbling and thus salutary for proud sinners. Others have pointed to the therapeutic benefits of confession, the sense of psychological relief that results from disclosing one's failures to a trustworthy listener.

In my opinion neither of these "defenses" gets to the theological heart of the matter. Ultimately, the purpose of avowing sin is neither humiliation nor therapy. Instead, its purpose is to move penitents forward toward the achievement of that identity in Christ which is mediated through the church as the eschatological symbol of reconciled humanity. Permit me to develop this point a bit further.

The Introduction to the new rite of penance identifies two levels of mediation ("ministry") in the church. The first is the ministry that belongs to the entire baptized community: "The whole Church, as a priestly people, acts in different ways in the work of reconciliation which has been entrusted to it by the Lord."[4] The second is the responsibility that belongs to ordained persons in the community: "The Church exercises the ministry of the sacrament of penance through bishops and presbyters."[5] These mediating levels of ministry are not opposed to one another, nor are they "ranked" in terms of "higher" versus "lower." Their relationship is seen as complementary, not as contradictory.

But the question arises: why bother with such "levels of mediation" at all? Why can't the sinner simply and humbly turn to God in his heart, thus avoiding all the fuss and hassle? To answer this question we need to recall what was said earlier in this essay about the nature of sin as self-estrangement, flight from oneself. Sin is more serious than mistaken judgment or bad taste; it is a radical rupture in the sinner's identity which results in the terrifying premonition that "I no longer know myself," "I have become a stranger to myself." When this happens, as I have argued, identity can be recovered only through the mediating power of symbols. As such a symbol, the church (reconciled humanity) acts to mediate to the sinner both recognition of sin (alienation) and promise of hope (the cosmic vision of a world reconciled through Jesus' cross). Indeed, as I have suggested earlier, it is only because the whole church stands as the symbol of such ultimate hope that the sinner is empowered to recognize the self-estrangement caused by sin. As the real symbol of reconciled humanity, the church empowers sinners to recover their identity as members of the Easter-Community. The moment when sin is avowed becomes, at the same time, the moment of eschatological hope in the power of Jesus' resurrection.

But what of the "second level" of mediation, the responsibility that belongs to ordained persons in the community? The interpersonal transaction between penitent and minister also derives its significance from the symbolic nature of the church. To confess one's sins to another is to relinquish the absurd project of being "master" of one's own life; it expresses a desire for life together as brothers and sisters in a reconciled humanity. By abandoning all pretension of "mastery," of willful domination, the confession of sin to another becomes a death to the "estranged self." The death of this "self" becomes an emptiness which can receive and be filled with an other, with the Other of reconciled humanity, with the Other of the resurrected Lord.

Thus the penitential avowal of one's sins to a representative of the community is a death to "self" (a false, unrecognizable self) for the sake of a being-with-others, a finding of oneself in others. The act of confessing expresses the penitent's willingness to receive a new self beyond this death, a self constituted by the eschatological symbols of the church, the community of the resurrection. The result is a reversal of the estrangement produced by sin. Sin had caused the penitent to become an incomprehensible puzzle ("I no longer know myself"); confessing to another empowers the penitent to recover his identity, to know himself again by being-with-others in a church which symbolizes reconciled humanity.

The death to self that results from the act of confessing is nothing less than love. This love is *limitless* because it arises, ultimately, from that "eschatological horizon of hope" discussed earlier in this essay; it is *concrete,* because it happens through an *interpersonal transaction* (dialogue between penitent and minister) in an *historical* community (church). The love that floods the penitent's heart in the act of confessing derives its power from the church's central symbol: the dead and risen Lord, the glorious Son of Man, the One whose blood "speaks" in the church and creates a new humanity. Jesus' death is the irreversible symbol of a love that is limitless, selfless and creative. The penitent's death to a false self in the act of confessing permits such love to take possession of his heart. One is reminded of George Herbert's description of the effect of Easter on sinners:

> Lord, who createdst man in wealth and store,
> Though foolishly he lost the same,
> Decaying more and more,
> Till he became
> Most Poore:
> With thee
> O let me rise
> As larks, harmoniously,
> And sing this day thy victories:
> Then shall the fall further the flight in me.[6]

The love that emerges in the act of confessing confirms the paradox Herbert hints at in the final line of this stanza: "Then shall the *fall further the flight* in me."

Absolving. In an earlier section of this essay I suggested that the formula of absolution in the new rite begins by opening the penitent's eyes

to a cosmic vision of reconciled humanity: "God the Father of mercies
. . . has reconciled the world to himself." Here, I should like to deal with
the second part of the absolution formula: "I absolve you from your
sins, in the name of the Father, and of the Son and of the Holy Spirit."
This declaration corresponds to an interpretation of the minister's office
as "judge." Indeed, the Introduction to the new rite comments that the
minister's office requires "a spiritual judgment by which, acting in the
person of Christ, he pronounces his decision of forgiveness or retention
of sins in accord with the power of the keys."7 In the light of all that
has been said thus far, what can a statement like this one mean?

There can be little doubt that the author(s) of the Introduction describe the minister's actions as juridical, as declarations of acquittal or
non-acquittal based on the penitent's avowal of sins. But a problem arises
here. On the one hand the penitent is required to appear before an external "tribunal" presided over by a minister/judge who "renders a verdict" based on what he has heard. On the other hand, the penitent faces
the interior tribunal of his own conscience, which demands that he accept personal responsibility for his actions. What is the relationship between these two "tribunals"? Does the minister/judge merely confirm
the verdict of the individual's interior conscience? Does he "correct" or
"overturn" the verdict of conscience, acting on the assumption that "nobody is a fit judge for his own case"?

Once again, this is a problem that has been debated by theologians for
centuries. St. Augustine, for example, appealed to the biblical story of
Lazarus in order to defend the importance and legitimacy of the minister's declaration of pardon. According to Augustine's exegesis, the sinner (= "Lazarus") is forgiven (= "raised from death") as soon as God
moved his heart to repentance; but the sinner remains *bound* (as Lazarus
was by the burial cloth) until the church's minister has formally declared
pardon. The exegesis is perhaps dubious, but it allowed Augustine to
make his point: no one is fully restored to communion with the church
until a qualified minister has officially announced pardon.

Ingenious as it may be exegetically, Augustine's position seems to
miss the real significance of the minister's role in absolving. If we recall
that the ultimate purpose of confessing is to move the penitent toward
recovery of identity in Christ, then we may also discover a basis for the
minister's action in the prayer of absolution. As a significant "other" in
the community, the minister acts to prevent the "interior tribunal" of
the penitent from collapsing in on itself in a hopeless welter of accusation and verdict, isolation and despair. Left to himself, the penitent can
be overwhelmed by the accusation of his own conscience. Like a char-

acter out of Kafka, he can find himself simultaneously accuser, judge and hangman—anonymously condemned by a self he no longer recognizes. To prevent this, the public action of the minister serves to maintain the bond between the *individual's* guilt and the *whole community's* sinful condition. The minister thus establishes a vital link between the *individual penitent* and the *penitential community*. His declaration of absolution serves public notice that the bond of fellowship in the community—sinner to sinner, penitent to penitent—remains alive and strong.

But the minister's action is not limited to maintaining good "socio-political order" in the community. The Introduction to the new rite insists that the "judgment" rendered by the minister is *"spiritual*," that the minister *"acts in the person of Christ."* This point should not be overlooked, for it suggests that the "tribunal" of the sacrament is a *symbolic* reality. The "tribunal" in question is not an earthly forum where cases are heard and tried according to the forensic model of civil courts. Rather, by "absolving," the minister acts to put the penitent in touch with the "eschatological judgment" of the Son of Man—the judgment that inaugurates the full and final reign of the risen Lord in a new humanity. The juridical language of the sacrament—"tribunal," "minister/ judge," "accusation/verdict"—must therefore be understood as *metaphoric*. What is at issue is not the minister's practical competence to "try cases" but the penitent's relation to Jesus, the "eschatological Judge" whose death and resurrection has passed final verdict on the world. A few comments about this last point may be useful.

Among the varied (and sometimes conflicting) christologies of the New Testament, one finds the image of Jesus as "Son of Man," "Judge," "King." This Son of Man is understood to render a judgment on the world that is final, definitive ("eschatological"). The result of such judgment is a New Creation, a New Era of pardon and peace to which all humanity is invited. Even though this New Creation is not yet fully revealed, its ultimate power is already at work in the world, challenging people to repentance, conversion and decision for the kingdom. To this figure of the Son of Man another image is joined—that of the Suffering Servant. When combined, these two figures—Son of Man, Suffering Servant—produce a curious result: the powerful eschatological *Judge* is one who is *willing to suffer,* to *give his life,* to *plead for all humanity* as a body. Matthew's gospel adds a further dimension to this picture: the Suffering Son of Man identifies himself with the lowly (Matthew 25:40) and with those on whom the "beatitudes" are pronounced (Matthew 5:1-12).

How this symbol of the Suffering Son of Man came to be applied to Jesus in the course of editing the New Testament need not concern us here. What is of crucial importance is that the faith of the early disciples in the death and resurrection of Jesus, who has become Lord and Christ, found its meaning in the fusion of eschatological symbols I have just described. Jesus, dead but risen to unsurpassable life, is the Suffering Son of Man, the Victim/King whose cross and resurrection is the *verdict of acquittal that arrives at our justification.* As his sinful death under the curse of the Law is transformed into an abundance of Justice which far outstrips the curse, so the acquittal of a penitent who "confesses" and is "absolved" by a "minister/judge" results in the incorporation of sinners into the Body of the Suffering Son of Man, into the community of reconciled humanity. It is this incorporation into a humanity that has been acquitted, justified and reconciled in Christ that gives the sinner access to forgiveness.

The Grace of Reconciliation with the Church

"He has sent the Holy Spirit among us for the forgiveness of our sins." These words from the prayer of absolution in the new rite will serve as the starting point for the final section of this essay, which explores the meaning of "reconciliation with the church."

Perhaps we can begin this exploration by indicating what reconciliation with the church does *not* mean. It does not mean the restoration of some *status quo,* the balancing out of some lost equilibrium. In light of what has been said about the nature of avowing sins and absolving sinners, reconciliation with the church cannot mean "making satisfaction," "restoring order" or "making restitution." For the purpose of the sacrament is not to render human judgments about the penitent but to put the sinner in touch with the "eschatological judgment" of Jesus the Lord and Suffering Son of Man. This judgment, as we have seen, is an *acquittal* that results in our justification, in the creation of a new humanity. Even if this new creation fails to register fully in our consciousness, even if its presence can be detected only as an "undertow," the fact remains: Jesus, as Judge of a New Age, has acquitted humanity of its guilt. Reconciliation with the church, like forgiveness of sins, must therefore mean participation in this acquittal, incorporation into a New Creation, a New Humanity. This is what the rites and symbols of sacramental penance ultimately strive to reveal.

Moreover, what is true for individual penitents is true of the entire historical community (church). It is the community, after all, which celebrates the rite of penance/reconciliation. Its action can never be reduced to a mere redressing of wrongs or restoring of order, for such a reduction would turn the sacrament into a political tool for keeping "offenders" and "undesirables" in line. That, of course, would transform the church from a "resurrection community" to a "totalitarian state" supported by ideology, coercive power and police-monitoring of behavior. "Good order," whatever its value, is not the purpose of reconciliation. Sinners are reconciled with the church not in order to "clean up the mess" but in order to release the power of the Spirit: "He has sent the Holy Spirit among us for the forgiveness of our sins."

The Spirit's action in forgiving sins thus becomes the sign that a pilgrim community is making its way home. "Home" is not a dreamy Camelot, distant and unreal, nor is it the present historical community with all its scabs, scars and minor successes. "Home" is New Humanity in Christ—real and powerful, even if only partially noticeable. This new humanity is not a wishful projection created by devious theologians to calm pangs of despair; it is what has been revealed in the broken and risen body of Jesus. It was that breaking of the Lord on the cross that released the power of the Spirit on all humanity. Similarly, it was the release of this power that made a new humanity simultaneously *possible* and *actual.* And finally, it is this new humanity that makes it possible for the church to come home. This "home-coming" is, at the same time, the full achievement of the church's identity as resurrection community, as "sacrament of grace in the world," as "reconciled humanity." Seen in this way, the church's identity is not something "still to be dreamed up in God's mind"; it is "already at home." Like the "Great Dance" of C.S. Lewis' *Perelandra,* the identity of the church "has begun from before always." And the sign that this is true is the Spirit's action in reconciling sinners.

That is why it is both possible and necessary for a *sinful community* to reconcile sinners. How can this be? What advantage is there, after all, in bringing sinful people back into a sinful community? Ordinary logic would regard this project as absurd. But there is another logic at work here: a logic of human imagination, a logic of symbol, rite and metaphor. The Spirit testifies to its presence in the community by working on that community's imagination, allowing it, *daring* it to put things together that don't seem to belong together—things like "sinful" and "holy," "guilty" and "just," "*no* people" and "*my* people," "humanity" and "God." The Spirit bestows on the community the power of metaphor, the power of symbol. For that is what symbols and metaphors do: they put things together that don't seem to belong together. This logic of the imagination is not fanciful; it is real—as real as Easter, as real as the furious fire of Pentecost that burns but never destroys. The Spirit forgives by allowing both penitent and community to *re-imagine,* to re-interpret human life in terms of wholeness and integrity, pardon and love. For, as the novelist Lawrence Durrell has reminded us, "the so-called act of living is really an act of the imagination." Life-giving and grace-bestowing, the Spirit forgives by making it possible once more for human persons to *imagine, really,* a reconciled life, a life where the self-estrangement of sin gives way to the achievement of identity in Christ.

Traditionally, we have called this Spirit-laden act of imagination "grace." Its source is the explosive possibility of the death and resurrection of Jesus; its signs, in Paul's words, are "love, joy, peace, patience, kindness, goodness, faithfulness, gentleness, self-control" (Galatians 5:22). It is to this logic of the imagination that the sacrament of penance/reconciliation appeals through its rites and symbols. The "grace" of the sacrament "works" by challenging the creative imagination of believers to embrace any evil or any death unreservedly, thus striving to transform it by love into an abundance of life which far exceeds the threat posed. The result of this striving can only be *freedom*—freedom for both penitent and penitential community. This freedom brings everyone home to the new creation, for it is nothing less than a life of tenderness for each other groaning in unlimited, incomprehensible love in one great act of giving birth to the "children of God" (see Romans 8:18-25).

Notes

1 *Perelandra.* New York: Macmillan Company, 1965, p. 214.

2 *Rite of Penance.* Washington, D.C.: United States Catholic Conference Publications, 1975, p. 5.

3 *Fallible Man.* Chicago: Henry Regnery and Co., 1965, pp. 156-161; 186-191.

4 *Rite of Penance,* p. 5.

5 *Ibid.*

6 "Easter Wings," from *The Metaphysical Poets.* Edited by H. Gardner. Baltimore: Penguin Books, 1972, p. 121.

7 *Rite of Penance,* p. 3.